Netting Your Ancestors

Genealogical Research on the Internet

Netting Your Ancestors

Genealogical Research on the Internet

Cyndi Howells

Published by Genealogical Publishing Co., Inc.
1001 N. Calvert St., Baltimore, MD 21202
Second printing 1997
Third printing 1998
Library of Congress Catalogue Card Number 97-73445
International Standard Book Number 0-8063-1546-6
Made in the United States of America

Table of Contents

Acknowledgments

I would like to thank several people who graciously shared their time, their resources and their knowledge of the subject so that I might complete this book. Each of the following people work tirelessly to provide the genealogical community with invaluable online research tools:

Karen Isaacson, ROOTS-L List Maintainer, Webmaster and Co-Owner of the RootsWeb Genealogical Data Cooperative (**http://www.rootsweb.com/**). Karen spends thousands of hours of her free time taking care of the online needs of genealogists all over the world. She is an incredible inspiration, showing us how we can make the Internet a tremendous research instrument.

John Fuller and Christine Gaunt, Co-Owners of the *Genealogy Resources on the Internet* web site (**http://users.aol.com/johnf14246/internet.html**). John and Chris are very dedicated to making Internet genealogy resources readily available to online researchers. Their web site and their friendship are treasured.

Jared Reimer, System Administrator for Sense Networking, in Seattle, Washington (**http://www.oz.net/**). Jared's help and terrific customer support is greatly appreciated, as is that of the entire Sense Networking staff. My web site and my knowledge of the Internet wouldn't be what they are today without Jared.

Myra Vanderpool Gormley, CG, syndicated columnist Los Angeles Times Syndicate. Myra's advice, support and friendship helped to make this project a reality. Before I knew her, she provided me with genealogical guidance through her column, and once I met her in person she gave me advice and tips that only a true professional could give. I couldn't have done it without all of the encouragement from Myra.

Last, but most important of all, I am more than thankful to my wonderful husband, Mark. His unending support, patience and willingness to fold laundry are a very small part of how he encouraged me to become a published author. Without Mark, this book would never have been started, much less finished. Thank you for seeing in me something I never dreamed I could become.

Cyndi Howells
July 1997

Foreword

The explosion of genealogical data on the Internet did not begin with a big bang. Rather, like wet kindling, it took a while for the spark to catch and finally hiss and sputter into existence. Now it is a roaring fire, blazing across the world and leaping over artificial boundaries.

For those of us who have pioneered in this field, it is exciting to watch as the rest of the world discovers the promise of unlimited access to information and of being able to make contact with cousins around the globe while we sit in the comfort of our homes. In just a few years many electronic gadgets we once considered toys — remote controls, telephone answering devices and garage door openers — have become commonplace items in our homes. You learned to use them, and you can learn to use a computer and a modem.

Like all technology, the World Wide Web is not perfect, nor will you be able to do all of your genealogical research with the click of a mouse. Nevertheless, getting online will allow you to discover genealogical sources and finding aids beyond your wildest dreams. New databases are being compiled daily and made accessible online. For those of you who are unable to travel to faraway repositories or whose responsibilities require your presence at home, the Internet will entertain and educate, plus it will enable you to make new friends.

Cyndi Howells has an outstanding web site. She has compiled links to thousands of genealogical· and historical-related sites that she has explored, and in the process she has learned how to navigate, find shortcuts, and avoid detours. She has a knack for teaching and has the ability to explain clearly without using technical jargon what many, wrongfully, believe is a difficult and complicated subject. It is not. The problem is that guides to the Internet are usually written by technical experts, with no background in genealogy. Howells, on the other hand, is a genealogist as well as a technical expert. She can teach you to "surf the 'net" to find the treasures you seek.

Myra Vanderpool Gormley, CG
Syndicated columnist Los Angeles Times Syndicate
May 1997

Introduction

In recent months, using the Internet for genealogical research has become overwhelmingly popular and the number of genealogists online has grown at a rapid pace. The ability to exchange information quickly and efficiently from your own home computer is the greatest innovation in genealogy since the advent of the personal home computer. Using the Internet for genealogical research has opened up a whole new world of tools that are only a keystroke away. Genealogists now have the ability to make their own research available to the entire world. They can communicate with other researchers and genealogical resource centers worldwide in a more rapid and less expensive manner. The world has become a much more accessible place and genealogical research is now very easy to manage on a global scale.

However, a number of genealogists still have many basic questions about online research: How do I get online? What type of computer software and hardware do I need? What do I do once I am online? Where do I start? What type of information is available?

In this book I will explain what tools you will need in order to get started online. I will also explain the ins and outs of using the most popular and most useful components of the Internet in order to help you maximize your online research time. These components are each represented in a separate chapter of this book as follows: e-mail or electronic mail, mailing lists and newsgroups and the "web" or World Wide Web. Within each chapter you will find information for those who are new to online research, as well as a lot of tips which will benefit researchers who have already been online for a time. The various sections detail software requirements, guidelines and basic usage of each component. There are also many helpful hints and bits of advice, which are designed to save you time and effort while researching on the Internet. The last section in each chapter is devoted to research strategies that will benefit both new and veteran online researchers. Don't be intimidated by the technical jargon throughout the book, because I will explain various terms as I go along and there is a glossary of terms and phrases at the back of the book for further reference. You will also find many examples and addresses for various Internet resources throughout the book. The addresses were current at the time of the printing of this book; however, with the ever-changing world of the Internet, I cannot guarantee that the addresses will remain unchanged.

The first question most people ask when they begin wondering about genealogical research on the Internet is, "What can I find online?" Many people begin their journey onto the Internet with rather high expectations, hoping to find simply everything they could ever dream of to complete their genealogy without ever leaving their house. While that may be a possibility in the very distant future, it isn't yet a reality. Instead, the Internet should be viewed as a brand new tool to add to your existing set of genealogical resources, on which you can do the following:

❖ Use the Internet as you would a genealogy collection at a library by reading through other researchers' genealogical information that they have posted on their personal home pages.

❖ Visit some web sites which have searchable databases from a variety of different resources, such as the Social Security Death Index, cemetery listings, military records, obituaries, some census records, surname lists and GEDCOM indexes and many, many more.

❖ Browse through library card catalogs online from the comfort of your home. These libraries could be right across town or all the way across the country or around the world. Plan a research trip to a library before you go!

❖ Contact people anywhere in the world and receive replies as quickly as the same the day. Your e-mail connection via the Internet is an easy and inexpensive alternative to using postal mail, the telephone or the fax machine.

❖ Use the Internet as you would a bulletin board system, genealogy newsletter or magazine where you can post queries and questions about your research. You can join genealogy mailing lists and newsgroups that focus on specific topics of genealogical research, so that your questions and queries can be discussed with other genealogists who are working in the same areas of research as you are.

❖ Find valuable tutorials, helpful articles and how-to guides on the Internet. Having these resources available to you in your own home makes it possible for you to gain the knowledge that you might otherwise only obtain at a genealogy conference or workshop. There are numerous resources online to help you learn about genealogical research in other countries and cultures, as well as many other specialty areas in genealogy.

◆ Use the Internet as your own personal online library of genealogy reference books. Visit sites with map collections online, genealogical dictionaries and glossaries, including those for foreign languages, directories of addresses for genealogical and historical societies, details for obtaining copies of vital records and many more resources of this type.

◆ You no longer need to worry about possible limitations when contacting people regarding your research. The Internet breaks down the traditional barriers of borders, distance and time zones. It also eliminates the inaccessibility of various archivists, librarians and genealogical experts, thus opening many more avenues for you to explore in your research.

◆ Find vendors online with a variety of genealogical products available for sale. You can order catalogs from vendors or browse through their catalogs online. Purchase books, CD-ROMs, charts, forms and supplies online.

◆ Download genealogy software demos so that you can try out a genealogy program before making a purchase. You can also learn about software in order to make comparisons, then buy the software and purchase software upgrades while you are online.

What You Will Not Find on the Internet for Genealogy

The potential for the types of resources that may be available on the Internet in the future can be mind-boggling at times. Currently, however, there are many things that you won't find while "surfing the 'net."

◆ You will not find your completed, personal family history online. Instead, you may connect with relatives and other researchers who are working on various lines in your family.

◆ Currently, there are not complete sets of birth, marriage or death records online. However, some online volunteers have begun to put a few of these records online for specific areas in their personal research. You can also visit sites that will give you helpful details, such as addresses and fees, so that you can obtain vital records through traditional methods.

◈ The International Genealogical Index® (IGI), Ancestral File™ or LDS Family History Library Catalog™ files are not online. These are records made available by The Church of Jesus Christ of Latter-day Saints (LDS) and their Family History Library located in Salt Lake City, Utah. Currently, they have no plans to put any of their holdings on the Internet due to privacy and expense issues. You will find many resources, however, that explain how to best use the LDS Family History Library's collection and you can also find copies of their very useful Research Outlines to aid you in your research strategies.

◈ There aren't any complete sets of census records online, although there are now many sites that have extractions of specific portions of census records or census indices. Each day more and more census material is being added to the web. You will also find many helpful guides to help you learn how to use census records and where to find census records and related resources.

Summary

The resources that are available on the Internet are increasing and expanding rapidly each day. This will only add to the list of possibilities for researching your family's history online. The Internet is not a replacement for any of the other important resources we use, such as libraries, archives, county records offices, bookstores, your local LDS Family History Center, etc. However, it is an extremely powerful tool because it brings resources from around the world right into your home through your computer and phone line. Making contacts with other researchers using the speed of e-mail and being in daily contact with other genealogists and their research materials make the Internet a valuable tool that is well worth learning about and exploring. From the comfort of your home, you will save yourself time and energy while broadening the scope and depth of your research. Now that you know what you will and will not find on the Internet, you can prepare and organize your research in order to determine the best strategy to use to coordinate your online and offline research efforts. The information in this book is designed to help prepare you to use the Internet as your newest and most versatile genealogical research tool. Now, shall we find out how you can begin *Netting Your Ancestors*?

Chapter I

Stepping Out
onto the Internet

The Tools You Will Need to Get Online: Computer Hardware and Software

Once you have made the decision to go online and give the Internet a try, you will need to be sure that you have the right computer hardware and software for your journey into cyberspace. The following details the *minimum* necessary requirements for your computer to be able connect to the Internet. However, I highly recommend that you use the most powerful and most current equipment and software that you can afford to buy. This will make your experience on the Internet as quick, easy and hassle-free as possible.

Hardware

You will need to have a working telephone jack near your computer or an extra-long telephone cord to reach the nearest jack. If you are sharing the line between your computer and your telephone and have call waiting, be aware that there are ways of disabling call waiting while you are online. By doing this, your Internet connection won't be interrupted by an incoming telephone call during an online session.

IBM-PC Compatibles: Hardware
You will need at least a 486 processor, running at a speed of 25 MHz or faster. A Pentium would be preferable. It is possible for a 386 to run the necessary programs, but the response time will be extremely slow and it will have difficulty handling all the graphics and multimedia effects that a web browser and many web sites have to offer.

Macintosh: Hardware
Either the Power PC or 68040 series of processor chips will work well.

Hardware for Both Types Of Computers

❖ You should have a minimum of 8MB of RAM, although 16MB and higher would be preferable and would make your life easier in the long run.

◈ Your modem should have a speed of at least 14.4 kbps; however, the higher speeds are definitely worth the extra money. I would strongly recommend a modem speed of 28.8 kbps or higher.

Software

IBM-PC Compatibles: Operating System and Utilities

◈ You need to be running Windows 3.1 or better.

◈ You should use a virus scanner program regularly, such as Microsoft's Anti-Virus that comes with Windows 3.1 or McAfee Virus Scan for Windows 95.

◈ For some files that you download, you will need to uncompress or *unzip* them with a program such as PKZip or WinZip, which are available for download at:

> ◈ **PKWARE, Inc.**
> http://www.pkware.com

> ◈ **WinZip Home Page**
> http://www.winzip.com

Macintosh: Operating System and Utilities

◈ You need at least a System 7.1 or higher operating system.

◈ You will need a virus scanner program, such as the shareware package called Disinfectant.

◈ You will also need to uncompress some of the files that you download by using a program such as Stuffit-Expander. This utility program and the Disinfectant program mentioned above are both available for download at:

> ◈ **Macintosh Internet Software Updates**
> http://www.tidbits.com/iskm/iskm-soft.html

Internet Software Programs for Both Types of Computers

There are three basic options for obtaining Internet software. The first two options listed below are for direct Internet access. The third is for accessing the Internet via a commercial online service such as America Online. See the list of commercial online services and Internet Service Providers in the next section titled "Getting a Direct Internet Connection."

1. There are Internet starter kits or books available in many computer software stores, bookstores, office supply stores and discount warehouse clubs. These kits include all of the software programs and manuals you will need to get started online. Many times they also include pre-loaded account information for Internet Service Providers (ISPs), along with a set of free hours to get you started. They also have an option that allows you to load the information for an ISP with which you have already started an account. Some of the more popular kits for Windows are Netscape Navigator Personal Edition and MS Internet Explorer Starter Kit. For Mac users, there are The Internet Starter Kit for Macintosh and The Apple Internet Connection Kit.

2. If you have already chosen an ISP, check with them to see if they will provide the software that you need to get started. Most of the programs they give you might be unregistered shareware or freeware, so this option is obviously the least expensive and the quickest way to get online. Once you are online, if you wish to change the programs you are using you can purchase one of the ready-made kits mentioned above or you can search for other software that is available for downloading from various sites on the Internet. See Chapter VI for addresses to many of these online sites.

The three basic pieces of software you will need for direct Internet access via an Internet Service Provider are:

A) A dialer software program which you use to dial-up your Internet Service Provider and makes the initial connection from your computer to the server at the ISP.

PC Users: Windows 95 comes with a dialer resident in the program. Windows 3.1x users need a TCP/IP stack package such as Trumpet Winsock, a shareware program which is available for download at:

◈ **Stroud's Consummate Winsock Applications**
http://cws.wilmington.net/

◈ **Tucows - The Ultimate Collection of Winsock Software**
http://www.tucows.com/

Mac Users: MacTCP and MacPPP come with more recent versions of the Mac operating system software. MacTCP comes with System 7.5. You can also obtain a copy of this program from your ISP if they have a site license from Apple. The Internet Starter Kit for Macintosh and other software packages on the market come with MacTCP and MacPPP. There are a few different versions of MacPPP available for downloading at:

◈ **Macintosh Internet Software Updates**
http://www.tidbits.com/iskm/iskm-soft.html

◈ **The Well Connected Mac**
http://www.macfaq.com

B) A web browser software program, such as the Netscape Navigator for Windows or Macintosh, which is available for download at:

◈ **Netscape**
http://home.netscape.com/

Or Microsoft Internet Explorer for Windows or Macintosh, which is available for download at:

◈ **Microsoft Corporation**
http://www.microsoft.com

C) An e-mail software program. Many web browsers come with e-mail features resident within the program, so a separate e-mail program is not necessary. These types of e-mail programs can be more limited in options and technical ability than a stand-alone e-mail program would be, so if you have a high volume of e-mail traffic, I would suggest using a separate program such as Eudora Light, a freeware program which is available for download at:

◈ **Eudora - A Division of Qualcomm**
http://www.eudora.com/

3. The third option available for accessing the Internet is to use one of the commercial online services such as America Online (AOL), Prodigy or CompuServe. These services provide all of the software that you need in order to get online with them. They also give you the web browser that you will need in order to access the Internet using their *gateway*. To use one of these services, you first dial in and sign on to their private network and then you can access the Internet from there. This means that the commercial services are an intermediate junction between you and the Internet. Because of this, your access time may be a bit slower than if you were to use a direct connection with an ISP. These services also provide the ability to send and receive e-mail anywhere on the Internet, not just to subscribers of that service. The commercial online services are a great place for beginners to start their trek onto the Internet and provide new users with the convenience of easy-to-use software and a variety of additional interesting features, including genealogy forums with expert online genealogists to help with questions. Some services offer a limited number of hours for a set fee, with additional hours online being charged at a separate hourly fee. Others offer unlimited time for a flat rate. For Internet users who plan to use more than the minimum number of hours offered by these services, the additional expense of a per-hour charge can become quite costly. I would suggest that after initially getting your feet wet with a commercial online service, you might consider switching over to a direct Internet connection with an Internet Service Provider in order to save a bit of money.

Commercial Online Services That Offer Internet Access:

◈ America Online   1-800-827-6364   http://www.aol.com
◈ CompuServe   1-800-524-3388   http://world.compuserve.com
◈ Prodigy   1-800-PRODIGY   http://www.prodigy.com

Getting a Direct Internet Connection

Once you have gone over your computer hardware and software needs, you will need to decide on an Internet service that best fits your needs. The following is a list of Internet Service Providers. The listed services and prices were current in June 1997. You should call each of these service providers first to confirm their current prices and account features. This list is merely a compilation of national ISPs that I could find with reasonable rates and services, as well as dial-up access nationwide. I do not endorse any one specific service. The prices and features I have noted below are for accounts within the United States, although I have indicated some ISPs that offer services in other countries as well.

Check your yellow pages for local ISPs in your area. If you can locate a computer with access to the Internet and the web · through a friend or a public library · you can visit a great web site which lists ISPs, their telephone numbers, services, prices and more. Search this site by city, state or the area code of your home telephone number:

◈ **The List**
   http://www.thelist.com

When looking for an Internet Service Provider you want to find the best account options available. Use the following list as a guideline when shopping for an ISP:

◈ Unlimited Internet access for about $20 a month.
◈ Local dial-up telephone number to avoid long-distance charges.
◈ Full Slip/PPP access.
◈ Modem speeds of 28.8 kbps and higher.
◈ No setup or start-up fees.
◈ Complete set of software to get you started online.
◈ Technical support available, preferably 24 hours a day.
◈ Free personal home page of 1MB · 5MB in size.

AT&T WorldNet Service
1-800-WORLDNET   http://www.att.com/worldnet

- ◆ AT&T long-distance customers can pay $4.95 for 5 hours a month or $19.95 a month for unlimited Internet access.
- ◆ Non-AT&T long-distance customers can pay $4.95 for 3 hours or $19.95 a month for unlimited Internet access.
- ◆ AT&T WorldNet Service Kit software available for Windows or Macintosh.

Concentric Network
1-800-939-4262   http://www.concentric.net

- ◆ $19.95 a month for unlimited Internet access.
- ◆ Software package available.
- ◆ Toll-free technical support.
- ◆ A personal web page up to 5MB in size.
- ◆ Available in the U.S. and Canada.

Earthlink Network
1-800-395-8425   http://www.earthlink.com

- ◆ $25.00 setup fee, $19.95 per month for unlimited Internet access.
- ◆ TotalAccess complete software package for Windows and Macintosh.
- ◆ Telephone and online technical support.
- ◆ A personal web page up to 2MB in size.

The Microsoft Network
http://www.msn.com

- ◆ Available only to Windows 95 users. One month is free.
- ◆ $19.95 a month for 20 hours of Internet access, additional hours are $2.00.
- ◆ Telephone and online technical support available.
- ◆ Available in the U.S., Canada, Australia and Japan.

Mindspring
1-800-719-4332   http://www.mindspring.com/

- ◈ Start-up fee $25.00.
- ◈ $19.95 for unlimited use, no web space.
- ◈ $26.95 for unlimited use, 10MB for personal web/FTP space, 2 extra mailboxes.
- ◈ Telephone and online technical support available.
- ◈ Software available for Windows or Macintosh.
- ◈ Available nationwide in the U.S.

Netcom, Inc.
1-800-NETCOM1   http://www.netcom.com

- ◈ Unlimited access for $19.95 a month.
- ◈ NETCOMplete suite of Internet software for Windows and Macintosh.
- ◈ Telephone and online technical support available.
- ◈ A personal web page up to 1MB in size.
- ◈ Available in the U.S., Canada and the United Kingdom.

Sprynet
1-800-SPRYNET   http://www.sprynet.com

- ◈ $19.95 per month for unlimited Internet access.
- ◈ A software starter kit for Windows and Macintosh.
- ◈ Telephone and online technical support available.
- ◈ A personal web page up to 5MB in size.
- ◈ Available in the U.S., Canada, France, Germany and the United Kingdom.

Installing the Software

Now that you have opened an account with a service provider and have obtained all of the necessary hardware and software, you are ready to install the software programs to get connected.

❖ Before you run the install routine, follow all of the vendor instructions in the manuals and read-me files. Be sure to read any specific instructions given to you by your Internet Service Provider or commercial online service.

❖ Run the install or setup routine and enter the appropriate details and information as you are prompted to do so by the program.

❖ Be sure that your modem is turned on. Then start up the commercial online service program or if you have a direct ISP connection, start up the dialer program. Dial-in to the Internet service and be sure that the modem makes a successful connection.

❖ Once online with the commercial online service, move around within the various menus and windows to determine that the program is working correctly.

❖ Once online with the direct Internet connection through your ISP, minimize the dialer program (leave this program running in the background) without turning off the connection. Start the web browser program and watch to see that it is working properly and that the default home page loads.

Chapter II

Communicating Online
with E-mail

E-mail: The Most Important Tool in Online Genealogical Research

In online genealogy, e-mail is the most important tool for researchers to utilize. In order to make the most of this powerful component of the Internet, you need to take the time to get to know everything you can about using e-mail. This means you need to be familiar with the various options in your e-mail software program, as well as the general basics of e-mail use in the online community. This chapter will cover all of that and more.

E-mail or electronic mail was one of the first applications developed for use on the Internet. It allows users to send electronic messages to other Internet and computer network users by using an Internet connection. In using e-mail, you can send messages at the speed of a telephone call, yet save the cost of long-distance charges. When sending a message, you don't need to worry about what time of the day or night it is as you would with a telephone call. You can compose and send the e-mail message at your convenience and it will be received and downloaded by the other person at his or her convenience. It is also possible to save expenses by using the option of attaching a computer file to an e-mail message. You won't need to purchase blank floppy disks and spend money on postage to mail copies of your GEDCOM files or other computerized genealogy files to other researchers. E-mail is an inexpensive, quick and efficient alternative to postal mail, long-distance telephone calls and copies of documents sent by fax machine.

For genealogists, making contacts by e-mail can be much more rapid than the traditional waiting that we have always done with *snail mail*, also known as postal mail. It is very easy to copy bits and pieces of your family information from your genealogy software program and then paste it into an e-mail message to share with someone else. E-mail is a very simple way to share information and to stay up-to-date with other researchers who are working on the same family lines or in the same areas that you are working in. Hundreds of institutions such as libraries, universities and genealogical or historical societies now have e-mail addresses. This allows you to request information, directions or other types of help and advice from them in a quick and efficient manner, without the wait time or long-distance charges involved in traditional methods. In this chapter I will explain what tools, tips and techniques you will need to know about in order to effectively use e-mail to communicate with a variety of genealogical resource contacts online. See also Chapter III, "Mailing Lists and Newsgroups," for more information on utilizing e-mail in your online genealogical research efforts.

The Tools You Will Need For Using E-mail

There are four components that you will need to have in order to begin using e-mail:

1. A connection to the Internet via an ISP or commercial online service.

2. A dialer software application for your computer. Windows 95 comes with a dialer resident in the program. Windows 3.1x users need a TCP/IP stack package such as the shareware program, Trumpet Winsock. Macintosh users need MacTCP and MacPPP. These programs come with more recent versions of the Mac operating system software.

3. Space on your computer's hard drive or extra floppy disks for storing copies of incoming and outgoing e-mail messages that you may want to keep for future reference.

4. An e-mail software program for your computer. There are many different e-mail software programs available today:

    ◈ Commercial programs can be purchased at any computer software retailer.

    ◈ Commercial online services such as AOL, Prodigy and CompuServe have an e-mail function resident within their software.

    ◈ Some web browsers also contain e-mail programs that are resident within the browser program itself.

    ◈ Shareware or freeware programs are obtainable from your ISP or by downloading them from a web site. See Chapter VI for more web site addresses with software and shareware programs like these.

◈ Once you are well established in your online research, you may find that you have a high volume of e-mail traffic. In this case, for more flexibility, I would suggest using a separate, stand-alone e-mail program such as my favorite, Eudora Light. This is a freeware program for Windows or Macintosh which is available for download at:

◈ **Eudora - A Division of Qualcomm**
   http://www.eudora.com/

Getting to Know Your E-mail Program

When you have successfully installed and started up your e-mail program, you should familiarize yourself with the various menus, features and options available.

The e-mail program that I currently use is Eudora Pro for Windows. Most of the examples, tips and techniques that I will talk about are based on my knowledge of that program and my prior use of Eudora Light. However, many e-mail programs work very similarly and have the same basic functions, so you will be able to apply these examples to whatever e-mail program that you choose to use.

◈ Refer to your software manual, help files or the directions received from your Internet service in order to set up the appropriate technical information regarding your Internet account, as well as your own personal details and preferences.

◈ Learn how your program allows you to create a new message, reply to an incoming message, send outgoing mail and check for incoming mail.

◆ The e-mail program will have an **In** box and an **Out** box in which copies of all incoming and outgoing e-mail messages are stored. Each individual message within these boxes is generally labeled with the name and/or e-mail address of the sender or receiver, the date and time that the message was sent and the text of the subject line for that e-mail message. To open an e-mail message in either the **In** box or the **Out** box, place your cursor over the line of the message and click with your mouse, or follow the instructions in your e-mail program for other methods.

The Format and Layout of an E-mail Message

An e-mail message consists of the body of the message and several fields at the top contained in the *header*.

Example of a new, outgoing e-mail message in Eudora Light.

The header fields are generally as follows:

 To:

Fill in this field with the e-mail address of the person to whom you are sending the e-mail message.

◈ Be sure to type in the e-mail address **EXACTLY** as it is given to you. For example, if the address is shown in all lower-case letters, be sure to use all lower-case letters. If some are upper-case letters and some are lower-case letters, be sure to type them exactly as shown.

◈ Some Internet computer servers read and interpret e-mail addresses with case-sensitive character sets. For example, if you incorrectly type an e-mail address with an upper-case *A* rather than a lower-case *a*, the e-mail message may bounce or become undeliverable and you will have to re-send the message with the correct address.

Helpful Hint

Whenever I am able to, I use the highlight, copy and paste function to input an e-mail address, rather than type it out manually. This helps me to avoid errors in typing and results in fewer undeliverable or bounced e-mail problems.

◈ It is only necessary to fill in an e-mail address in the **To:** field; however, some e-mail programs will allow you to fill in a "real name" as well. For example, if you were going to send an e-mail to me, you could either fill in my e-mail address as:
> **cyndihow@oz.net**

or you could fill in my real name and e-mail address like this:
> **Cyndi Howells <cyndihow@oz.net>**

Note that you must place angle brackets on either end of the e-mail address to enclose it and separate the address from the real name.

◈ It is possible to fill in more than one e-mail address in the **To:** field.

Type in each individual address and separate them from one another with the correct character required by your e-mail program. Some programs use a comma and a space. Other programs use a semicolon. Read the e-mail program's documentation to learn which character to use.

From:

This field will contain at least your e-mail address and should also include your "real name."

◆ During the initial software and account setup process, you will supply the e-mail program with your basic user information. Once you have done this, the information in the e-mail program on all outgoing messages automatically fills in the **From:** field.

◆ Visit the options or preferences menu of your software program in order to input or edit your real name, e-mail address and return or reply-to address. This information is included in the header on all of your outgoing e-mail messages.

◆ The return or reply-to e-mail address and your name which are stored in the header of your outgoing message will also be used in the reply feature of the e-mail recipient's software program. When others receive an e-mail message from you, they will use the reply button or menu feature on their own program to compose an e-mail reply back to you. If you have properly supplied your e-mail program with the correct information, you won't have any problems receiving responses to your e-mails. If you did not supply the correct user information in your e-mail program options menu, return e-mail messages to you will bounce and you won't receive replies to any of your e-mail correspondence. Even the smallest error or the omission of a single character will prevent others from successfully replying to your e-mail messages.

Subject:

The **Subject:** line in an e-mail can be a very important tool in successful e-mail communications. This is especially true when you participate in genealogy mailing lists (see Chapter III).

◆ Type in a short, but clear and concise, subject line for your message. In using an explicit and clean-cut subject line, you will increase your chances of having someone take the time to read your message and perhaps even reply to it.

◆ Some Internet users have e-mail programs that limit the number of characters that are displayed in their e-mail **In** box, sometimes to as few as 30 characters. This means that you need to make each letter and number count when composing a well-written subject line.

◆ When responding to another person's e-mail message, you choose the **Reply** feature on your toolbar or menu. Most e-mail software programs will automatically insert in the subject line *RE:* which stands for "Regarding." The programs will also insert the sender's original subject line. By doing this, the person receiving your reply will know that you are sending a response to one of his or her specific messages.

◆ If your e-mail program requires you to manually type in a subject line for messages that you are replying to, be sure to type in the *RE:* and repeat the sender's original subject line.

◆ A great example of a clear, concise subject line for a genealogist to use in order to best convey his meaning would be one like this:
JONES, Edward 1850-1884 Johnstown, Cambria Co, Pennsylvania
This is a clearly composed subject line because it includes a surname in capital letters; a first name; specific dates; and a specific location including a town, county and state. The length of this subject line is under 70 characters, which is the maximum width that many e-mail programs will display. Since some programs display as few as 30 characters, try to keep your subject to this length whenever possible.

⬛ Cc:

In order to send copies of an outgoing e-mail message to several people, you can use the **Cc:** field.

◆ Type in each person's e-mail address and their "real name" if known, separating each entry with the appropriate character, such as a comma or a semicolon.

◆ The **To:** field is used for the main recipient of your message, while the

---

Cc: field is used to send copies to other people who need to be aware of the information being shared by the sender and the receiver.

❖ An example of when you might use the **Cc:** feature is if you are posting or replying to a genealogical query. In the body of the e-mail message, you would be communicating with the main recipient of the message. You would then use the **Cc:** field to send copies of this message to friends, relatives or associated genealogists who are working on the same family lines or project. This enables you to share contacts and potential discoveries without a lot of duplication of effort by everyone involved.

Bcc:

The **Bcc:** field is used for sending a *blind copy* of an outgoing e-mail message to a third party. You would use the blind copy function if you are sending a message to someone and you also wish to send a copy of that message to another person without informing the main recipient that you have sent out copies to anyone else. When the main recipient of your e-mail message receives the message, there will be no indication in the header on the message that the blind copy feature was used. Follow the same format guidelines as mentioned above for the **Cc:** field.

Attachments:

The **Attachments:** field is used to indicate the name of a computer file that has been attached to an e-mail message.

❖ Use the appropriate toolbar button or menu item to attach a file to an outgoing message. Follow the options you are presented with to indicate which disk drive, directory and file name you wish to use.

❖ Once you attach a file to an e-mail message, send the message as you would any other outgoing e-mail.

❖ During the transmission of your e-mail, you will notice that the attached file is in the process of being *uploaded*. This means that the computer file you chose for the attachment is being copied, attached to the e-mail message and moved to your ISP's server. The upload process can take a bit of time, depending on the size of the attached file and the speed at which your modem connects your computer to your ISP's server. With larger files, be prepared to wait for a while until the upload process is complete.

❖ After you have uploaded the message and the attached file to your ISP's server, it is forwarded through the Internet to reach its destination.

❖ When the person receiving your e-mail message signs on to his service and attempts to download the incoming e-mail, he will encounter the same or similar wait time while the attached file downloads from his ISP's server to his home computer. The amount of time that he has to wait for the download to finish will depend on the file size and the speed at which his modem and computer communicates with his ISP's server.

❖ As a courtesy, you should always ask people if they are willing to receive an attachment via e-mail before you send it to them. Some Internet users are charged by the time that they spend online, so large attachments can become expensive for them to download. Also, users in rural areas may have to pay long-distance telephone charges for their Internet access.

❖ Another good practice, which I strongly urge you to set up as a routine, is to **ALWAYS** check attached files that you receive via e-mail with your computer's virus scanner software program before you attempt to open or use the file.

❖ There are several types of files that online genealogists might choose to share with others by using an e-mail attachment:

1. GEDCOM files converted from their genealogy software database.
2. Scanned image files such as family photos, old documents and other family heirlooms.
3. Miscellaneous genealogy files such as notes, lists, charts and other research materials.

❖ See further ideas regarding attachments below in the "How to Send and Receive E-mail Messages" section.

📫 Date:

The **Date:** field in the header will be filled in automatically by the

---

e-mail program, which uses the date and time that is currently set on your computer's internal clock. All incoming e-mail messages will indicate the date and time that the messages were sent from their place of origin. All of your outgoing e-mail messages will indicate the date and time that you sent the messages.

Body:

Use the body of the e-mail to type out your message. Compose e-mail messages in the same way that you would write a letter.

◆ Begin with a salutation such as, "Dear Mr. Smith."

◆ Check the name that is signed at the bottom of an e-mail you are replying to, because it isn't always the same as the name that appears in the **From:** field. An example of this would be on joint accounts where several family members use the same e-mail address.

◆ For queries or questions that you are asking:

    a)   Be specific in your message and clearly state what the information is that you are trying to find out about.
    b)   Clearly state what you already know about the topic.
    c)   Define what it is that you hope the person at the other end might be able to help you with.

◆ For answers or replies to others:

    a)   Cite any sources you have used in order to find the answer for this person.
    b)   Clearly separate your personal opinion from any stated facts.
    c)   Address each question or topic individually.
    d)   Quote text from the original message, in order to respond to specific statements. Many e-mail programs will automatically quote an entire message when you use the return or "reply to" feature. The quoted text will appear in the body of the message with a right-pointing caret bracket appearing at the beginning of each line of text, as in the following example:

>Dear Mr. Smith,
>I am also researching the JOHNSON family from Tisbury,
>Massachusetts and would like to learn more about your
>family line. Please e-mail me with the names and dates
>regarding your JOHNSON family....

◈ Whenever you have more than one topic or question, break up the information into separate paragraphs to make each subject stand out. Doing this helps people who only read through or scan an e-mail message very quickly. They are more likely to address each of your points if you have distinguished them individually.

◈ Be specific and supply the recipient with names, dates, places and other helpful details.

◈ Don't ever assume that the person at the other end knows the same things that you know about the topic.

◈ Always capitalize any surnames that you are including in the message. This makes the names easier to pick out as a message is read.

◈ All text, other than surnames, should be typed using proper punctuation and capitalization.

◈ End with an appropriate closing such as, "Sincerely yours."

◈ After the closing, be sure to type out your name and e-mail address, as well as any other identifying information that you might like to add.

**See* *the* "Tips and Techniques for Successful E-mail Communications" *section for more ideas on composing e-mail.*

How to Send and Receive E-mail Messages

Now that you have become familiar with your e-mail software program and with the format of an e-mail message, you are ready to start communicating with your "cyber-cousins" online.

Sending E-mail

1. Open your e-mail software program.

2. Open a new, blank e-mail message by clicking on the appropriate toolbar button or menu option. Compose a new outgoing e-mail message following the guidelines in the section above on e-mail layout and format.

3. Ask a friend who is online if you can send him your first e-mail so that you can practice with all of the features of the e-mail program. Make sure that your friend sends back a reply so that you can also be sure that all of your user information has been correctly entered into your e-mail program's options and preferences.

4. Dial-up your connection to the Internet.

5. Send your completed e-mail message by using the appropriate button on the toolbar or the menu option for sending mail.

6. Once the message is sent, it will be stored in the **Out** box in the e-mail program. The date and time that the message was sent will be noted, along with the subject line and the name and e-mail address of the recipient.

1.   Open your e-mail software program.

2.   Dial-up your connection to the Internet.

3.   Use the appropriate toolbar button or menu option for checking, receiving or downloading e-mail.

4.   All incoming e-mail messages will be stored in the **In** box in the e-mail program. Each message that is received is listed on an individual line. The date and time that the message was sent will be noted, along with the subject line and the name and e-mail address of the sender.

5.   To open and view a message, place your cursor over the line of the message and click with your mouse. Or follow the instructions in your e-mail program for other methods.

6.   Read your messages and reply to any of them that interest you. Most e-mail programs will allow you to both read incoming mail and compose your outgoing e-mail while offline. By doing this you can save actual online time and expenses.

7.   After sending and receiving all of your e-mail messages, disconnect your Internet connection. If you are using a separate dialer and e-mail program, you can close the dialer application and continue to use the e-mail program while offline.

Helpful Hint

Make it a routine to check your incoming e-mail at least once a day. There is a limited amount of space available to you for e-mail messages on your Internet service's computer or "server." If you don't download your incoming e-mail regularly, you run the risk of having the space fill up. If that happens, any new incoming messages may not be accepted and will be returned to the sender.

File Attachments

You can attach a file to an e-mail message so that it can be transferred from your computer along with the e-mail you are sending. The person who is receiving the e-mail can then download it at the other end. You can send a variety of different types of files, including zipped files, text files or graphic files (i.e., scanned photographs). An example of the type of file that genealogists would most likely send would be a GEDCOM file. If you find someone online that you would like to compare information with, you can send him or her an e-mail message describing what the file is and attach the appropriate GEDCOM to the e-mail, then send it. When the person receives the e-mail with the attachment, his e-mail reader program will automatically download the file and deposit it into the specified directory on his computer's hard drive. The receiver can then open the file and read it with the appropriate software program. In the example of a GEDCOM file, he would import that file into their genealogy software program to read it. For a text file, he could open it in his word processor program.

To attach a file using Eudora for e-mail, open a new outgoing e-mail message. Choose **Message** on the menu bar, then choose **Attach File**. You will then be able to choose the directory name on your computer, followed by the name of the file that you wish to attach to the message. Once your choice is made, click the **Open** button. You will now see the name of your directory and file in the **Attached:** field in the header of your e-mail message. When you send this message the attached file will be uploaded along with all of your outgoing e-mail.

Compressed or Zipped Files

When sending someone a file attachment that is made up of a large file, you may decide to compress or *zip* the file to make it more compact, thus quicker to send and download. In the opposite situation, you also may receive an attachment that is a zipped file. You will need to *unzip* the file before you will be able to view it in the appropriate software application. Usually these compressed files end with the extension *.zip*. Zipped files can be made up of any type of computer file or group of files, which have been run through a special program that codes and compacts the files to make them smaller in size. There are several types of shareware programs available to zip or unzip files (see list below). Be sure to obtain a copy of one of these programs, so that you are prepared for the opportunity to send or receive a file that is compressed. The documentation that comes with the zipping programs will tell you how to use them in order to zip or unzip a file.

◈ **PKWare, Inc., for PKZip Shareware**
http://www.pkware.com/

◈ **WinZip Home Page**
http://www.winzip.com/winzip_x.htm

◈ **Stuffit and Stuffit Expander for Macintosh**
http://www.aladdinsys.com/

◈ **ZipIt**
http://www.awa.com/softlock/zipit/zipit.html

Tips and Techniques for Successful E-mail Communications

One of the best things about using e-mail is that it makes communications with other researchers happen very quickly, while ignoring traditional concerns over time-zone differences, long-distance charges, etc. E-mail is convenient and inexpensive to use. This means that people are more apt to stay in touch with friends, families and associates who live far away. They are very likely to write more often and drop a quick note here or there as they find spare time.

While the speed and efficiency of e-mail is one of its outstanding attributes, it can also be one of the drawbacks if the people who send and receive the e-mail do not use clear communication methods. Quite often, people treat e-mail in a very casual way, much like a live conversation that they might have over a telephone. This is obviously due to the swiftness at which e-mail messages can be sent and replies received back · sometimes only in a matter of minutes! Many times you can pass a series of e-mail messages back and forth almost as quickly as you can make a series of telephone calls. When people are in a hurry, they tend to type a quick message and send it off. By doing so, it is possible to make assumptions about what the person at the other end knows or doesn't know about the topic. It is also possible that errors might be made in typing or in the facts being conveyed. The following are a few tips and hints that will help you to maintain the best e-mail skills, while taking advantage of this remarkable tool.

Be Careful What You Write

◆ Always use proper punctuation, capitalization and all other forms of clear communication.

◆ Use clear, concise and short subject lines that will grab the attention of other genealogists. Type surnames in all capital letters and include specific dates and places as well. It isn't necessary to say things in a subject line like "Researching...." or "Need help with..." because other genealogists will already be aware of that - that is what we are all here for after all!

◆ Be sure to proofread your message before you send it. Check for spelling and make sure that you have made your meaning and intent clear.

◆ Before replying to a message, be sure to read it carefully more than once. You want to be certain that you understand the message.

◆ When replying to an e-mail message, be sure to quote some of the text from the original message, so that you can show that you are responding to specific items in the e-mail. The quoted text will appear in the body of the e-mail with a right-pointing caret bracket at the front of each line of text. Many e-mail programs will automatically quote the text and insert the carets when you use the **Return** or **Reply** feature. It is not necessary to include the entire text of the original message, so you can edit out the portions that are not relevant to your reply.

◆ Don't abbreviate words or use slang terminology. Remember that your audience may be in another city, state, region or country. Everyday slang or jargon that may be familiar to you most likely won't be understood halfway around the world.

◆ When writing about locations such as cities, counties, states or countries, spell out the entire name. A person in England may not know that "WA" is the abbreviation for the state of Washington. After all, it is also the accepted abbreviation for Western Australia.

❖ The safest method of communication is to be sure that you never assume anything about your audience. They do not necessarily have the same knowledge that you do about a topic. They may not be following the same pattern of thought regarding a specific subject.

❖ As in all good communications, explain your motivations for sending the e-mail. Make all your details clear and ask specific questions. Make certain that you state exactly what it is that you hope to learn or gain from the person you are writing to.

❖ Remember that in not meeting someone face to face, you may miss many non-verbal clues and important body language. Because of this, you face the possibility of misunderstanding someone or having him or her misunderstand you.

❖ Whenever possible, don't send e-mail messages on a negative impulse. If you do feel the necessity to write to someone in an angry or critical manner, go ahead, but after you have written the message be sure to set it aside and DO NOT send it. Walk away, get your mind off of the situation and let the e-mail message sit overnight. You may want to re-read the original message that made you angry and re-read your own reply as well. If you still feel as strongly about it the next day, you can send the message if you like. However, many times the strong feelings you had about the topic disappear once you have had time to relax and think about it a bit. Keep in mind that once the message is sent there is no way to get it back.

❖ When writing to someone whom you have never met, try not to use sarcasm or humor, because it doesn't always translate well in the written form. It is very tempting to feel totally at ease when writing an e-mail message because you are safely tucked away in your home. You won't actually be meeting this person face to face, so any nervousness you might ordinarily feel when being introduced to a stranger for the first time seems to disappear. Keep your initial correspondence with a new online contact as polite and friendly as you possibly can. If you do use humor in your message, be sure to label it clearly as such. After you get to know someone well via e-mail, you will know what the comfort levels are on both sides and also where those invisible boundaries exist and whether or not they exist at all!

❖ There are several symbols commonly used in e-mail messages that help you to get across the idea of humor or other emotions. They are called *emoticons*. They are tiny pieces of artwork that you can see if you tilt your head slightly sideways, like a "smiley" face as in this example: :-)
Or a wink as in this example: ;-)   Please see the glossary at the end

of the book and look under the e-mail section for more examples of emoticons that you can use in your e-mail correspondence.

◆ There are dozens of acronyms that online e-mail users include in their e-mail messages each day. Internet users worldwide know these acronyms. Examples of these are: *BTW* - by the way, *FYI* - for your information, *IMO* - in my opinion, *<BG>* - big grin. Please see the glossary at the end of the book and look under the e-mail section for a list of acronyms that people use in their everyday e-mail correspondence.

Helpful Hint

I have a set of pre-written e-mail messages that I use in order to reply to repetitive questions. For example, when I receive general inquiries about my Dougherty surname, I use one of these messages to reply to the e-mail. My pre-written answer has a basic descendant outline list of my Dougherty line, a paragraph describing my current research efforts on this surname and a friendly salutation at the end encouraging the sender to contact me if they find any connections in our research. These messages save me time and duplication of effort. I encourage you to use a similar strategy in your e-mail.

Be Courteous in Your E-mail Messages

As you begin to send and receive e-mail messages, you will be making all sorts of new genealogical contacts and new online friends. It can be very different from most situations that you are used to because you may never meet these people face to face. Always keep in mind that you are corresponding with real, live people and not just a faceless computer. Basic rules of common courtesy should apply, as well as the following:

◆ Treat people with the same courtesy and respect with which you wish to be treated yourself.

◆ Always respond to an e-mail message as soon as possible, just as you would a telephone call. If you are busy and intend to reply in detail on a later date, just drop the person a quick e-mail message telling them what you intend.

◆ Be sure to send a nice thank-you e-mail to people who have responded to your query or request for help. Since this person has taken the time to help you, it is the least that you can do in return. Even a short, one or two sentence reply is better than no reply at all.

◆ When asking for help with a research question or a request for a lookup, you might want to offer a similar service in return, making use of your own personal resources and local resources such as libraries and genealogical or historical societies.

◆ Do not type messages in all CAPITAL letters. For people reading an e-mail, this is considered *shouting*. Capitalization should be reserved for when you wish to EMPHASIZE a word or a sentence. However, for genealogists, it is always appropriate to type surnames in all CAPS. It is also very helpful to do this so that people who are skimming through messages can pick out the names quickly and easily.

◆ Keep in mind that some people are charged fees by their service provider according to the number of e-mails they receive, the size of the e-mail files or even according to the time they spend online in order to download them. So keeping messages short, clear and concise will allow them to receive their e-mail in an economical manner.

◆ Always ask people before sending them overly large messages or file attachments to be sure that they are able or willing to receive them. Some people are still using older e-mail programs with formats that are unable to handle certain types of files or messages. Others who are charged by the time they spend online wouldn't want to download a file that would take quite a while and add expense to their monthly bill.

◆ When replying to an e-mail message, be sure to use only quoted text that is necessary to help with the context of your response. Your e-mail program may automatically quote the entire text of the original message. You should take the time to edit out any dispensable text to save space on the message and to make the message easier to read.

Miscellaneous E-mail Considerations

◆ Do not forward junk mail, also known as *spam*. This refers to multiple

---

copies of e-mail messages that are sent to numerous e-mail addresses, usually for business or advertising purposes.

◈ Do not forward chain letters or messages with warnings of viruses. These are usually just a hoax that is meant to cause a flood of e-mail to unsuspecting online users.

◈ Learn everything you can about your e-mail software program. The more you know about it, the more successful your e-mail usage will be. Take advantage of all the options and features that the program offers to make the best use of your time spent on e-mail.

◈ **Andrew Starr's [Unofficial] Eudora Site**
http://www.amherst.edu/~atstarr/eudora/eudora.html

◈ **Computer Virus Myths**
http://www.kumite.com/myths/

◈ **Don't Spread That Hoax!**
http://crew.umich.edu/~chymes/Hoaxes/Think.html

◈ **Fight Spam on the Internet**
http://spam.abuse.net/spam/

◈ **Internet Navigator - Communicating Over the Internet**
http://www.lib.utah.edu/navigator/email/email.html

◈ **U.S. Dept. of Energy Computer Incident Advisory Capability (CIAC)**
http://ciac.llnl.gov/ciac/CIACHoaxes.html

Research Strategies for Using E-mail

Each mailbox is actually just one long text file that generally ends with a .mbx file extension. It is possible to open and view this file in your word processor or any other text editor. When you do that, save the file with a new name and file type. You can then edit the file and clean out certain messages or unnecessary e-mail header information. This file can now be treated in any way that you like in order to use the information for your personal research. Perhaps you keep a notebook with possible surname connections for future reference. Or maybe you like to keep all geographical information about Germany or another locality. Use this trick to make your own research methods more efficient.

Signature Files

A signature file is a small text file that can be automatically attached to each e-mail message that you send out. A signature file or *sig file* should be no more than 4 or 5 lines long and no more than 70 characters wide. A sig file should at least contain your name and your e-mail address. It's a good idea to include your mailing or *snail mail* address as well, just in case your e-mail message is read by someone who cannot send an e-mail reply to you. It is, of course, optional to do so and you should only do so if you are comfortable sharing your address with the world. Signature files can also contain other personal information of your choice. Some people will put in their favorite quote or family motto. Others will include a bit of ASCII art, such as little comic characters or logos. Whenever you use a sig file, remember to be thoughtful of the people who are receiving your e-mails. You wouldn't want to include anything that might be offensive. You want to keep your signature file short and clear, not long or messy. Your e-mail software program should have an option for creating and storing a sig file within its menu choices.

For genealogists, an ideal use of the signature file is to list the surnames you are researching. You may want to list only the major surnames in your family or each of the surnames that you are currently researching. By doing this, each time you send an e-mail message, other genealogists can scan your list of surnames and contact you if they feel they may have a similar line of research. When sending e-mail to a large mailing list, like ROOTS-L, you should temporarily disable your sig file, per their guidelines. This way your signature file will not be included in your post to that mailing list. Also remember to disable the signature file when sending commands to a mailing list computer software program. Otherwise the computer program will try to interpret the extra text in the message and it will reject the command because it won't understand the extra text it encounters. Here is an example of what a typical signature file might look like:

```
~~~~~~~~~~~~~~~~~~~~~~~~~~~~~~~~~~~~~~~~~~~
   cyndihow@oz.net    ~~~    Genealogist Researching:
   Cyndi Howells      ~~~    Cartwright, Dougherty,
   Street Address     ~~~    Frederick, Ingle, Johnson,
   City, State, Zip Code  ~~~  Kenney, Knox, Nash,
   USA                ~~~    Sanderlin, Thomas
     http://www.oz.net/~cyndihow/
```

Determine what information you would like to include in your signature file. Create the file using your e-mail software program's appropriate option. Then send a test message to yourself. Once you receive the test message you will be able to see how the signature file appears in your outgoing messages. You can make alterations and adjustments to it based on your own personal preferences.

◈ **Signature Etiquette and a Signature Collection to View**
http://www.math.fu-berlin.de/~guckes/elm/elm.sig.etiquette.html

E-mail Forwarding

As genealogists, we want to be sure that we can be found when that long-lost cousin turns up. So we must do our best to set up forwarding addresses and make everyone aware of changes in address or phone number. Along those lines, an e-mail address is very important as well. Every time you leave a query on a web site or on a mailing list that ends up getting archived, you leave behind your e-mail address in the hope that someone, someday will find you. However, if you change your Internet Service Provider your e-mail address changes as well. Some services will forward e-mail for you for a short time, but not indefinitely. The solution? There are now e-mail services available which offer free e-mail, a permanent e-mail address or e-mail forwarding. You can set up a permanent e-mail address with one of these companies and no matter where you go, your address will never change (as long as that company is still around and in business!). I haven't used any of these services myself, so I can't really endorse any particular one. If you decide to give this idea a try, you may test the e-mail service for a while before actually beginning to post the e-mail address with your queries.

◈ **Juno**
http://www.juno.com/

◈ **HotMail**
http://www.hotmail.com/

◈ **RocketMail**
http://www.rocketmail.com/

◈ **NET@DDRESS**
http://www.netaddress.com/

◈ **NetForward**
http://www.netforward.com/

◈ **Yahoo! - E-mail Forwarding Services**
http://www.yahoo.com/Business _and_Economy/Companies/ Internet_Services/E-mail_ Providers/Forwarding_Services/

Chapter III

Mailing Lists and Newsgroups

Mailing Lists and Newsgroups

Now that you know all the essentials for successful e-mail communications, you are ready to use that information in order to participate in online discussions known as mailing lists and newsgroups. Mailing lists and newsgroups are groups of e-mail messages sorted by specific topics that can be accessed by people all over the world. These topics range from specific surnames to ethnic groups, localities worldwide, religious groups or specific historical events. Messages sent to mailing lists and newsgroups contain everything from general questions to surname queries, as well as requests for help, offers of help, advice, research hints and tips. You can browse, read and post messages, as well as respond to other messages contained in a mailing list or newsgroup and thus participate in ongoing "conversations," also known as *threads*. Participation in these forums is free and the only expense to you is the cost of your e-mail and Internet connection.

Mailing lists and newsgroups can be compared, in a fashion, to bulletin board systems and chat rooms. They are like a meeting place (although not in "real time," like live conversations) for people with interests in the same topics. Mailing lists and newsgroups make it very easy to find other researchers who are also doing work in your areas of interest. Genealogists can participate in the activities of a variety of different mailing lists or newsgroups (see the list of examples at the end of this chapter). By doing so, you can make new contacts and friends anywhere in the world. You can participate in discussions on specific areas of research and share research tips, hints and ideas with one another. You can post genealogical queries or lists of the surnames that you are researching and also scan similar lists posted by other researchers.

Mailing lists and newsgroups are very similar forums on the Internet. I am going to concentrate mostly on discussing mailing lists in this book because there are only about twenty newsgroups available for genealogy, while there are literally hundreds of genealogy mailing lists. To participate in a mailing list, you send an e-mail message to a computer that redistributes the message to all other subscribers on that mailing list. You also receive messages from the other subscribers of the mailing list in the same way. To participate in a newsgroup, you view the groups of messages with a newsreader software program and then send e-mail messages to the newsgroup to be added to the existing set of messages. That is really the only noticeable difference between the two forums. Whereas newsgroups require you to actively search out the messages of interest, mailing lists send messages to your e-mail address automatically, without effort on your part. Otherwise, the methods and procedures are basically the same for making the most of these wonderful research tools.

> **Don't be alarmed by the terms* subscriber *or* subscribe. *There are no subscription fees to join these mailing lists. Mailing lists and newsgroups are free to use. The term* subscribe *merely refers to the method of adding yourself to the list of people who participate in one of these forums.*

Choosing to use mailing lists versus newsgroups is something that is purely a personal preference. As I already mentioned, there are many more mailing list topics to choose from than there are available newsgroup topics of interest to genealogists. I prefer to use mailing lists because there are more available topics and also because of the convenience of automatically receiving messages that are sent to the mailing lists. That way I don't have to remind myself to visit a newsgroup in order to catch up with all of the current messages and threads.

Many of the newsgroups are *gatewayed* or *mirrored* with corresponding mailing lists. This means that the same e-mail messages will appear in both places, so that you may have twice as much exposure for any information or queries that you post. Most mailing lists and newsgroups have archives of all the previous messages that have been posted by users. These archived messages are quite often online and searchable, which means that it is possible to make connections or find useful information on something that was posted prior to your own venture onto the Internet.

Joining a mailing list or newsgroup that is specific to your line of research is one of the basic strategies for success in online genealogical research. By doing so, you give yourself a wonderful opportunity to utilize the power, diversity and convenience of the Internet.

The Tools You Will Need for Mailing Lists and Newsgroups

There are five essential components that you will need to have in order to participate in mailing lists and/or newsgroups:

1. A connection to the Internet via an ISP or commercial online service.

2. A dialer software application for your computer. Windows 95 comes with a dialer resident in the program. Windows 3.1x users need a TCP/IP stack package such as the shareware program, Trumpet Winsock. Macintosh users need MacTCP and MacPPP. These programs come with more recent versions of the Mac operating system software.

3. Space on your computer's hard drive or extra floppy disks for storing copies of incoming and outgoing e-mail messages that you may want to keep for future reference.

4. For mailing lists, an e-mail software program for your computer. The Netscape Navigator web browser and the commercial online services such as AOL, Prodigy and CompuServe all come with e-mail software resident within their program. See Chapter VI for more web site addresses for shareware and freeware e-mail programs.

5. For newsgroups, a newsreader software program for your computer. There are several different options available for newsreader programs:

   ❖ Some web browsers have newsreaders that are resident within the browser program itself. One example of this type of browser is the Netscape Navigator, available for download from the Netscape web site at **http://home.netscape.com/**.
   ❖ Commercial online services such as AOL, Prodigy and CompuServe have a newsreader function resident within their software.
   ❖ Use shareware or freeware programs that you can obtain from your ISP or by downloading them from a web site. See Chapter VI for more web site addresses with software and shareware programs like these.
   ❖ Purchase a commercial program at any software retail store.

Getting to Know Your
E-mail and Newsreader Programs

When you have successfully installed and started up your e-mail program and/or your newsreader program, you should familiarize yourself with the various menus, features and options available.

The e-mail program that I currently use is Eudora Pro for Windows, **http://www.eudora.com/**. The newsreader program that I currently use is Free Agent for Windows, **http://www.forteinc.com/**. Most of the examples, tips and techniques that I will talk about are based on my knowledge of those programs. However, most e-mail and newsreader programs work very similarly and have the same basic functions, so you will be able to apply these examples to whatever program that you choose to use.

◆ Refer to your software manual, help files or the directions received from your Internet Service Provider in order to set up the appropriate technical information regarding your Internet account, as well as your own personal details and preferences.

◆ Learn how your e-mail program allows you to create a new message, reply to an incoming message, send outgoing mail and check for incoming mail (see Chapter II).

◆ The e-mail program will have an **In** box and an **Out** box in which copies of all incoming and outgoing e-mail messages are stored. Each individual mailing list message within these boxes is generally labeled with the name of the mailing list that the message was sent to, along with the name and/or e-mail address of the sender or receiver; the date and time that the message was sent and the text of the subject line for that e-mail message. To open an e-mail message in either the **In** box or the **Out** box, place your cursor over the line of the message and click with your mouse. Or follow the instructions in your e-mail program for other methods.

The Eudora Light E-mail program with an example of the In box, the Out box and a new, outgoing message.

◈ Learn how your newsreader program allows you to subscribe to and view newsgroups, post new messages to newsgroups, reply to newsgroup messages and check for new sets of messages in specific groups.

◈ Become familiar with the newsreader program's set of three windows used to display the information. The upper-left window lists the newsgroups alphabetically by name. The list can comprise either the entire set of newsgroups that is available to you through your ISP or it can be set to show only those newsgroups to which you have "subscribed." You can highlight your choice of newsgroup in this list. The upper-right window lists in date and time order all of the current messages and *threads* that are available for the newsgroup you have highlighted and selected in the window on the left. A thread is a series of ongoing conversations resulting from the posting of a specific message. The window on the bottom displays the contents of the message that you choose from the list in the upper-right window. You

---

can view one message at a time in this window. You have the ability to print the message, reply to the message or create a new message in this window as well.

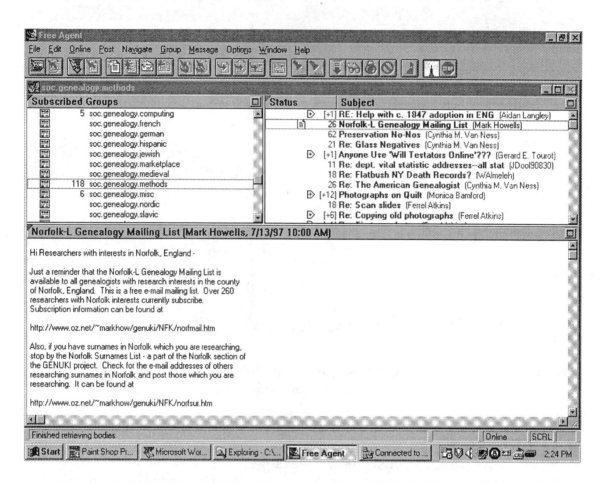

The Free Agent newsreader program with examples of the list of newsgroups currently being subscribed to, the list of subjects available for one specific group and a copy of a post to that same newsgroup.

How Mailing Lists and Newsgroups Work

A mailing list management software program runs the mailing lists, which are in turn maintained by a person known as a *listowner* or *list manager*. A listowner is responsible for making sure that users of the mailing list are properly subscribed *to* or unsubscribed *from* the list, as well as a variety of other maintenance duties. There are several types of software programs that manage mailing lists, including LISTSERV, SmartList, MAISER, ListProc and Majordomo. Each of these programs has a different set of parameters and commands that make it operate, but the manner in which they work is generally the same.

Each mailing list has two e-mail addresses associated with it. The first e-mail address is used to send "commands," such as *subscribe* or *unsubscribe*, to the list's mailing list software program. The second e-mail address is used to send actual messages to the list in order to have that message distributed to all other subscribers on the list. So in one case you are "talking" to the computer to maintain your subscription and in the other case you are posting your text messages, thus "talking" to the other human beings participating in the list discussion. Be sure to pay strict attention to the differences between these two e-mail addresses, so that you know you are using the proper address for the proper function.

When you find the mailing list subscription details that you need in order to subscribe to a specific list, be sure to follow the instructions exactly as written. If you aren't careful with the subscription command, the message will bounce and cause extra work for the listowner. Once you've successfully subscribed, be sure to keep a copy of the welcome message which contains the subscription information. By doing this, you will be able to correctly manage your subscription in case you ever want to unsubscribe, order copies of messages, temporarily stop delivery of the messages or any other of a variety of possible mailing list command options.

Once you become familiar with the various menus and features of your e-mail software program, you are ready to access a mailing list and start *lurking*. Lurking refers to reading mailing list entries and learning the ins and outs of that group for a little while before you actually join in and begin posting messages yourself. By lurking, you can learn a lot about how mailing lists work, about *netiquette* and about what types of researchers are out in cyberspace with you.

How to Subscribe to a Mailing List

In order to subscribe to a mailing list, you send a *command* to the software program via e-mail. Each program works differently, so pay strict attention to the instructions given for each list.

1. Create a new, outgoing e-mail message.

2. In the **To:** field, fill in the e-mail address for the mailing list that is specifically for user commands and subscription maintenance.

3. In the body of the message, type in the command exactly as it is shown in the instructions you have for subscribing to this particular mailing list.

4. Be sure to turn off your signature file for this message or it will cause the command to fail.

5. Once you receive the welcome message or a file called a *FAQ* (frequently asked questions), be sure to read it thoroughly in order to familiarize yourself with all the rules and guidelines for the list. Save a copy of this message for future reference.

How to Unsubscribe from a Mailing List

In order to unsubscribe from a mailing list, you also send a command to the software program via e-mail. Each program works differently, so pay strict attention to the instructions you are given for the list from which you are attempting to unsubscribe. You will find these instructions in your original welcome message.

1. Create a new, outgoing e-mail message.

2. In the **To:** field, fill in the e-mail address for the mailing list that is specifically for user commands and subscription maintenance.

3. In the body of the message, type in the command exactly as it is shown in the instructions you have for unsubscribing from this particular mailing list.

4. Be sure to turn off your signature file for this message or it will cause the command to fail.

5. You will receive an e-mail confirmation that you have successfully unsubscribed.

Individual Messages or Digest Mode

Quite often you have two options for the format in which you would like to receive your mailing list messages. You can receive the messages in *single* or *mail format*, which means that throughout the day you will receive individual e-mails from each subscriber who posts messages to the list. The other option is to receive the messages in *digest mode*. The digest is a group of e-mail messages that is put together by the mailing list software program and sent to you in one long message. Usually there is an index at the top of the digest made up of the subject lines from each message contained. With lists that are heavy in e-mail volume, the digest mode would be the more preferable method. For example, the ROOTS-L mailing list is the largest genealogy mailing list on the Internet with over 8,000 subscribers. There are generally four to six digests each day and each digest will usually contain between 30 and 50 messages. If you were to receive these messages in single mail format, you would be downloading e-mail messages all day long! It is much easier to manage the messages in digest format because you can pick and choose which messages you will read and which messages you will simply ignore and skip over. Each mailing list is different, so they all may not have the digest option. Check with the list manager or the mailing list's welcome message to find out what options are available for the list in which you are interested.

```
From: ROOTS-L-request@rootsweb.com
Date: Day, Date, Month 1997 Time Sent to Subscribers
Subject: ROOTS-L Digest V97 Issue number
X-Loop: ROOTS-L@rootsweb.com
X-Mailing-List: <ROOTS-L@rootsweb.com> archive/volume97/issue
Reply-To: ROOTS-L@rootsweb.com
To: ROOTS-L@rootsweb.com


.............................

ROOTS-L Digest                    Volume 97 : Issue Number

Today's Topics:
#1 Subject Line        [Sender's name and e-mail address]
#2 Subject Line        [Sender's name and e-mail address]
#3 Subject Line        [Sender's name and e-mail address]
#4 Subject Line        [Sender's name and e-mail address]
#5 Subject Line        [Sender's name and e-mail address]

Administrivia:

This ROOTS-L digest has been distributed by RootsWeb. RootsWeb's
home page is at http://www.rootsweb.com/.

If you would like to unsubscribe from ROOTS-L, send to
ROOTS-L-request@rootsweb.com the message "unsubscribe" (without
the quotation marks). Don't include your address, your signature, or
anything in the message body except that one word. (Do this also
if you want to shift to NOMAIL mode, then just resubscribe later.)

If you would like to have a message included in the ROOTS-L digest,
send it to ROOTS-L@rootsweb.com.
.............................

X-Message: #1
Date: Day, Date, Month 1997 Time Sent to the ROOTS-L Mailing List
From: Subscriber's Name <e-mail address>
Subject: A well-worded description of the message

Hi all –

This is an example of a typical ROOTS-L mailing list digest. Each
digest has between 20 and 40 individual messages contained within.
ROOTS-L Subscriber, Your signature information
```

```
┌─────────────────────────────────────────────────────────┐
│                      Helpful Hint                        │
├─────────────────────────────────────────────────────────┤
│                                                          │
│  You can use the Find feature in your e-mail software    │
│  program to look for specific keywords, surnames or      │
│  topics of interest within each digest and within        │
│  each mailbox.                                           │
│                                                          │
└─────────────────────────────────────────────────────────┘
```

Examples of Subscription Details for Some Popular Mailing Lists

Following are examples of four mailing lists with full subscription details and descriptions. The instructions and e-mail addresses were all current at the time that this book was printed. If you find a problem with any of these instructions or addresses, be sure to see the "Newsgroups & Mailing Lists" category on *Cyndi's List* **http://www.oz.net/~cyndihow/sites.htm** for current details.

1. ROOTS-L

For broad-based, general genealogical discussions and queries. ROOTS-L is the first genealogy mailing list and it is currently the largest with over 8,000 subscribers to date. The mailing list is pre-screened, but not moderated. The pre-screeners weed out the misposted messages (mailing list commands, complete quotes of digests in a reply, etc.) from the mailing list before it is distributed. They do not censor messages, but do check to be sure that they fall within the ROOTS-L guidelines that are detailed in the welcome message.

To subscribe to the ROOTS-L mailing list:

1. Send an e-mail message to one of the following addresses:

   ROOTS-L-request@rootsweb.com   (for single messages)
   ROOTS-D-request@rootsweb.com   (for digest mode)
   ROOTS-I-request@rootsweb.com   (for index only)

2. In the body of the message, type only this one word: subscribe
3. Be sure **not** to use a signature file with this message.
4. Save a copy of the welcome message that you receive for future reference.
5. To post messages to the list for all subscribers to receive, send e-mail to:

ROOTS-L@rootsweb.com

To unsubscribe from the ROOTS-L mailing list:

1. Send an e-mail message to one of the following addresses:
   ROOTS-L-request@rootsweb.com   **(for single messages)**
   ROOTS-D-request@rootsweb.com   **(for digest mode)**
   ROOTS-I-request@rootsweb.com   **(for index only)**
2. In the body of the message, type only this one word: unsubscribe
3. Be sure **not** to use a signature file with this message.
4. You will receive a confirmation message showing that you successfully unsubscribed.

To view the archived messages for ROOTS-L and learn more about the most popular mailing list for genealogy, choose one of the following web sites:

◆ **The ROOTS-L Home Page**
http://www.rootsweb.com/
roots-l/roots-l.html

◆ **ROOTS-L Daily Index of Messages**
http://www.rootsweb.com/
roots-l/index/

◆ **Search the Archive of ROOTS-L messages from 1987 through present**
http://searches.rootsweb.com/
roots-l.search.html

◆ **ROOTS-L Resources:
Info and Tips for Using ROOTS-L**
http://www.rootsweb.com/
roots-l/rootshelp.html

2. GEN-NEWBIE-L

A mailing list where people who are new to computers and genealogy may interact using a computer's e-mail program. The list discusses genealogy, family history, computer applications and a wide variety of other topics. Members are very tolerant, with a goal of assisting anyone who wants "community coaching" about the Internet, genealogy, computers, or whatever.

To subscribe to the GEN-NEWBIE-L mailing list:

1. Send an e-mail message to one of the following addresses:
   GEN-NEWBIE-L-request@rootsweb.com   **(for single messages)**
   GEN-NEWBIE-D-request@rootsweb.com   **(for digest mode)**
2. In the body of the message, type only this one word: subscribe

3. Be sure **not** to use a signature file with this message.
4. Save a copy of the welcome message that you receive for future reference.
5. To post messages to the list for all subscribers to receive, send e-mail to:

> **GEN-NEWBIE-L@rootsweb.com**

To unsubscribe from the GEN-NEWBIE-L mailing list:

1. Send an e-mail message to one of the following addresses:

> **GEN-NEWBIE-L-request@rootsweb.com**   (for single messages)
> **GEN-NEWBIE-D-request@rootsweb.com**   (for digest mode)

2. In the body of the message, type only this one word: unsubscribe
3. Be sure **not** to use a signature file with this message.
4. You will receive a confirmation message showing that you successfully unsubscribed.

Also be sure to see this web site:

◈ **GEN-NEWBIE-L Home Page**
http://www.rootsweb.com/~newbie/

3. GENUKI-L

A discussion group among people researching ancestors, family members, or others who have a genealogical connection to any people in any part of the British Isles (England, Wales, Ireland, Scotland, the Channel Isles and the Isle of Man). This e-mail group is gatewayed with the soc.genealogy.uk+ireland newsgroup.

To subscribe to the GENUKI-L mailing list:

1. Send an e-mail message to one of the following addresses:

> **GENUKI-L-request@rootsweb.com**   (for single messages)
> **GENUKI-D-request@rootsweb.com**   (for digest mode)

2. In the body of the message, type only this one word: subscribe
3. Be sure **not** to use a signature file with this message.
4. Save a copy of the welcome message that you receive for future reference.
5. To post messages to the list for all subscribers to receive, send e-mail to:

> **GENUKI-L@rootsweb.com**

To unsubscribe from the GENUKI-L mailing list:

1. Send an e-mail message to one of the following addresses:
    GENUKI-L-request@rootsweb.com   (for single messages)
    GENUKI-D-request@rootsweb.com   (for digest mode)
2. In the body of the message, type only this one word: unsubscribe
3. Be sure **not** to use a signature file with this message.
4. You will receive a confirmation message showing that you successfully unsubscribed.

To learn more about the GENUKI-L mailing list for genealogy, visit either of the following web sites:

◈ **The UK + Ireland Genealogy Page - "GENUKI"**
http://midas.ac.uk/genuki/

◈ **Frequently Asked Questions for soc.genealogy.uk+ireland**
http://www.meertech.demon.co.uk/genuki/socguki.htm

4. GENNAM-L

For surname queries and tafels in order to help genealogists make contact(s) with people who are researching the same family lines. This is a moderated mailing list group, which is gatewayed with the soc.genealogy.surnames newsgroup. The format for posting to this mailing list and newsgroup is very strict, so please read the FAQ or carefully observe other posts before submitting your own.

To subscribe to the GENNAM-L mailing list:

1. Send an e-mail message to one of the following addresses:
    GENNAM-L-request@rootsweb.com   (for single messages)
    GENNAM-D-request@rootsweb.com   (for digest mode)
2. In the body of the message, type only this one word: subscribe
3. Be sure **not** to use a signature file with this message.
4. Save a copy of the welcome message that you receive for future reference.
5. To post messages to the list for all subscribers to receive, send e-mail to:
    GENNAM-L@rootsweb.com

1. To unsubscribe from the GENNAM-L mailing list:

2. Send an e-mail message to one of the following addresses:
   GENNAM-L-request@rootsweb.com   **(for single messages)**
   GENNAM-D-request@rootsweb.com   **(for digest mode)**

3. In the body of the message, type only this one word: unsubscribe

4. Be sure **not** to use a signature file with this message.

5. You will receive a confirmation message showing that you successfully unsubscribed.

To search the archived messages for GENNAM-L, visit the following web site:

◈ **Search soc.genealogy.surnames Posts**
   http://searches.rootsweb.com/sgsurnames.html

How to Create and Send New Mailing List Messages

1. Open your e-mail software program.

2. Open a new, blank e-mail message by clicking on the appropriate toolbar button or menu option. Compose a new outgoing e-mail message following the guidelines in the section in this book on e-mail layout and format. You should also be sure you are following the guidelines for the mailing list you are sending your message to.

3. In the **To:** field, fill in the e-mail address used for posting messages to other subscribers on the mailing list you are interested in. Be sure **NOT** to use the e-mail address used for commands to the mailing list software program.

4. Dial-up your connection to the Internet.

5. Send your completed e-mail message by using the appropriate button on the toolbar or the menu option for sending mail.

6. Once the message is sent, it will be stored in the **Out** box in the e-mail program. The date and time that the message was sent will be noted, along with the subject line and the name and e-mail address of the recipient.

```
┌─────────────────────────────────────────────────────────┐
│                    Helpful Hint                          │
├─────────────────────────────────────────────────────────┤
│                                                          │
│  See Chapter II of this book for more tips and hints     │
│  regarding how to compose your e-mail and mailing        │
│  list messages, giving particular attention to the       │
│  sections "Be Careful What You Write" and "Be            │
│  Courteous in Your E-mail Messages."                     │
│                                                          │
└─────────────────────────────────────────────────────────┘
```

How to Access Incoming Mailing List Messages

You can access mailing list messages in the same manner that you access any incoming e-mail messages.

1. Open your e-mail software program.

2. Dial-up your connection to the Internet.

3. Use the appropriate toolbar button or menu option for checking, receiving or downloading e-mail.

4. All incoming e-mail messages will be stored in the **In** box in your e-mail program. Each message that is received is listed on an individual line. The date and time that the message was sent will be noted, along with the subject line and the name and e-mail address of the sender.

5. To open and view a message, place your cursor over the line of the message and click with your mouse, or follow the instructions in your e-mail program for other methods.

6. Make it a routine to check your incoming e-mail at least once a day. There is a limited amount of space available to you for e-mail messages on your Internet Service Provider's computer or *server*. If you don't download your incoming e-mail regularly, you run the risk of having the space fill up. If that happens, new incoming messages may not be accepted and would *bounce* or be returned to the sender as undeliverable.

7. Most e-mail programs will allow you to read incoming mail and compose your outgoing e-mail while offline. By doing this, you can save actual

online time and expenses, while making sure you avoid having a busy signal on your phone line.

8. After sending and receiving all of your e-mail messages, you can disconnect your Internet connection if you like. If you are using a separate dialer and e-mail program, you can close the dialer application and continue to use the e-mail program while offline.

How to Read and Respond to Mailing List Messages

Each day you will receive several messages for each mailing list to which you are subscribed. The messages will come from other members of the mailing list. The header information in the e-mail message will indicate the name of the mailing list, the e-mail address of the sender and the subject line for that message. Incoming e-mail messages are stored in the **In** box of your e-mail program. You can open the messages and read them as you like, whenever you like. You are not required to respond to any of the messages unless you want to do so. When you are finished reading a message, you can reply to it, print it, delete it or transfer it to another mailbox in your software program for temporary or long-term storage. Many mailing lists have archives of all of their old messages, so it is usually possible to go back and search for specific messages or topics at a later date. Therefore, whether or not you keep copies of messages from a mailing list is a personal choice and preference.

◈ If you wish to reply to an individual mailing list message, you can use the **Reply** button on the toolbar or use the **Reply** menu option on your e-mail program. The reply function then quotes the entire original message back to the sender. The quoted message appears within the body of the new outgoing e-mail message, along with angle brackets > at the beginning of each line of text (see the following example). These brackets are there to indicate that this is quoted material. You can then type in your reply message and send the e-mail.

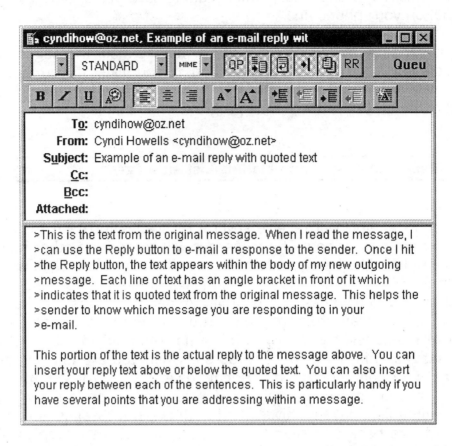

Example of an e-mail message with quoted text used to reply to the sender.

◈ When receiving copies of mailing list entries in digest mode (see page 61), if you use the reply feature you will end up replying to the entire mailing list and the whole digest is quoted and repeated in the outgoing message. This is not the polite thing to do, because the length of the e-mail is unnecessary and takes time to send and receive, as well as space to store. Here is a shortcut for replying to an individual person whose message appears within a digest:

a) Highlight the entire header and message of the e-mail you are responding to with your mouse. To do this, place the cursor in front of the first character you wish to copy. Click the mouse button and drag it across the text to just after the last character you wish to copy. Release the mouse button.

b) Choose **Edit, Copy**, then open a new, blank e-mail message.

c) Place your cursor in the body of the new message and choose **Edit, Paste** or if the option is available to do so, choose **Paste as a Quotation**.

d) Highlight, copy and paste the e-mail address for the person you are replying to in the **To:** section of your outgoing e-mail message header.

e) Highlight, copy and paste the subject line from the original message and add *RE:* in front of it in the subject line of your reply. *RE:* indicates that you are replying to a message previously sent by this person.

f) Add your own personal message within the body and send the e-mail.

g) If you wish to reply to the message, but also wish to post your reply to the whole mailing list audience, you would use this same method of copying and pasting the message as described above. Then you would fill in the mailing list address in the **To:** field, rather than the e-mail address of the individual person.

How to Access Newsgroup Messages

The first thing to do is dial-up your Internet connection, then minimize your dialer window in the background. You will use newsreader software to access messages in a newsgroup. There are at least three ways that you might access a newsgroup:

◈ You can manually type in the name of the newsgroup into your newsreader.

◈ If your web browser is capable of launching its own newsreader (i.e., Netscape), you can click on a hypertext link to a newsgroup from a web site you are visiting. For instance, on *Cyndi's List of Genealogical Sites on the Internet,* **http://www.oz.net/~cyndihow/sites.htm**, see the category titled "Newsgroups and Mailing List*s.*" You will find links set up on this page for each of the genealogy newsgroups, as well as a few other related topics. Click on one of the newsgroup links and your browser will launch the newsreader program and access that newsgroup. When you are finished you can close down the newsreader and go back to the web page to do more *surfing.*

Example of the Netscape newsreader that is resident within the browser program.

◈ The second option is to start up a separate newsreader program and subscribe to the newsgroups that you are interested in visiting regularly. In your newsreader program, to set up subscriptions, you will need to call up the list of all the newsgroups that your ISP carries. This is generally an option such as **Show All Newsgroups**. Scroll through the list to the section for the newsgroups that start with **soc.genealogy**. You will be given a list of about 20 newsgroups. Highlight the ones that you are interested in and subscribe to them. In Netscape, you will check a little box off to the right of the name of the newsgroup in order to subscribe. In another newsreader program, you may find the subscription option shown under a menu or as a button on the toolbar. Each program is different, so you may need to look around or use the **Help** function. Once you have subscribed to the newsgroups of your choice, you can remove the rest of the list by choosing an option such as **Show Only Subscribed Newsgroups**. From this point on, your newsreader program will keep track of what groups you have been to and what messages you have read. There are many options available in various programs for maintenance of your subscriptions, including retrieving unread articles, retrieving new articles, filtering certain topics or authors, purging articles and tracking specific threads. As I mentioned earlier, there are several different newsreaders on the market, so the options available are different depending on which reader you use. If you become a serious newsgroup user, you may want to explore the different programs available to find one suited to your needs and preferences.

How to Read and Respond to Newsgroup Messages

Once you become familiar with the various menus and features of your newsreader program, you are ready to access a group and start lurking. Lurking refers to reading newsgroup entries and learning the ins and outs of that group for a little while before you actually join in and begin posting messages yourself. By lurking, you can learn a lot about how newsgroups work, about netiquette and about what types of researchers are out in cyberspace with you.

As stated earlier, newsreader programs are generally divided into three windows:

◆ The upper left window shows the list of newsgroups you are able to access. Highlight the name of a newsgroup you wish to visit.

◆ The upper right window shows the *headers* of the messages in the newsgroup you are accessing. The headers usually show the name of the person who posted the article, the subject line or title of that article and the date and time that the article was posted. There are also symbols next to headers that will indicate if there are any responses to that article, which means that a thread is being developed. Click on the thread symbol and your newsreader will show you all the replies below the original header. If you find a header that interests you, just highlight it and double-click with your mouse.

◆ The message will appear in the third window at the bottom of your screen. You can scroll through and read the message and, if you wish to respond, you can choose an option in your newsreader to reply to the article or reply by e-mail. When you reply to an article, your response will be posted to the newsgroup for others to view. When you reply by e-mail, your response goes directly to the author of the message. See Chapter II for some tips and hints regarding how to compose your e-mail and newsgroup messages.

```
Original Subject Line
     RE: Original Subject Line      First Person to Reply
     RE: Original Subject Line      Second Person to Reply
          RE: Original Subject Line      Reply to the 2nd Person
     RE: Original Subject Line      Third Person to Reply
          RE: Original Subject Line      Reply to the 3rd Person
          RE: Original Subject Line      Reply to the 3rd Person
```

Example of a "thread" of conversation in a newsgroup.

Moderated and Unmoderated Lists

If a mailing list or newsgroup is moderated, all e-mail messages are first sent to a *moderator*. The moderator is a person who screens all the incoming messages to be sure that they follow the mailing list's guidelines and are appropriate to be posted to the mailing list or newsgroup. Once the messages are screened, they are passed on to the subscribers of the mailing list or newsgroup. For unmoderated lists, the e-mail messages go directly to the mailing list, without being pre-screened.

Tips and Techniques for Mailing List and Newsgroup Success

Also refer to "Tips and Techniques for Successful E-mail Communications" in Chapter II.

Getting Started

◇ First and foremost, remember that there are TWO e-mail addresses for every mailing list. One e-mail address is for sending commands to a computer that runs the mailing list software program. The other e-mail address is for posting messages that will be distributed to all other subscribers of the list. Always check the address you use carefully before sending a message.

◈ Always read the welcome message, the guidelines and the *FAQ* (Frequently Asked Questions) that are written for each mailing list. Be sure that you adhere to the list's guidelines and rules in all of your postings. Certain mailing lists have very rigid structures. For example, the subject lines for the GENNAM-L list must follow a very specific format. Save a copy of the welcome message for future reference.

◈ Always lurk before you begin posting your own messages to a mailing list or newsgroup. It is best to lurk until you feel comfortable joining in the activities of the list. Familiarizing yourself with the practices of a mailing list first can help you learn about accepted participation and save you from being *flamed* or chastised for inappropriate messages or behavior.

◈ Do not send a test message to a mailing list or newsgroup. These forums do work, so sending a test message will only cause you to receive unnecessary e-mail from people telling you that you shouldn't have sent the test message in the first place!

Writing a Message

◈ Be sure your messages are clear and concise. Follow a format such as the following and you will be successful in conveying your meaning:

        1. Have clear, concise subject lines.
           example: ARIS, Albert, 1879 Norwich, ENG>1931 Seattle, WA
        2. Describe what you already know.
        3. Describe what you've already done in your research.
        4. Describe what it is that you want to find out.
        5. Show surnames in all CAPITAL letters so they stand out.

◈ The subject line in a message plays a key role in successful communications. Many people these days are very busy and don't have a lot of time to spend sorting through numerous e-mail messages. In this case they may just skim through subject lines to find messages that interest them. Your subject line should be concise and detailed. Include a surname and/or place name, as well as a pertinent date. Doing so will ensure that your message will stand out from those that just say "Genealogy" or "My surnames." Make the subject line of your message

---

work for you!

◈ Be sure to sign your e-mail message with at least your name and e-mail address. Some e-mail software programs do not forward this information in the headers of messages. Therefore, it is important to include this information in the body of your message so people can contact you.

◈ Don't type your messages in all CAPITAL letters. This is considered "shouting" and if you do this someone will be sure let you know that it is inappropriate. The exception to this rule for genealogists online is that we like to see SURNAMES in all caps, so that they stand out amongst the text and make it easy to do a quick scan of the message for surnames of interest.

◈ You should carefully read and even re-read an outgoing message before sending it to the mailing list or newsgroup to be sure of its content and to make certain that the intent behind the posting is clear. Be positive that you are conveying your true meaning and that you are not leaving out any important details.

◈ You should also keep to the topic of a specific group or list. Posting something that doesn't belong on that list will only clutter it up and waste time for other members of the group.

◈ If you have more than one subject to discuss, send each subject in a separate e-mail message. This makes for less confusion for the readers and will ensure that you will receive replies to each post.

◈ Whenever possible, quote your sources. Indicate titles of books, web site addresses, library names or any other reference you have used. If you are answering a question, don't just say something like "Try the Seattle Library." Be sure to supply the e-mail address, web site address and/or mailing address for the library as well.

◈ When posting an e-mail address or the address for a web site, make sure that you have typed it correctly. Double-check the entire address for accuracy. Many times people will post to a mailing list in haste, then spend a lot of time afterwards answering e-mail from people who complain because the address given was incorrect.

Helpful Hint

*I have created extra individual mailboxes in my e-mail program for each of the mailing lists to which I am subscribed. Once I have finished working with a message, if I want to save the message for future reference, I can transfer it out of my **In** or **Out** box and into the appropriate mailbox for storage. I have created similar mailboxes for each of the surnames I work on in order to store incoming queries from other Internet researchers. Finally, I have separate mailboxes for each of my net friends with whom I correspond regularly. I keep all messages to and from my friends in these mailboxes and have found them quite handy to refer to when a question comes up at a later date.*

Replying to Messages

◈ Carefully read a message before you decide to reply to it. Be sure you understand the meaning behind the question or statements. Do not read a message in haste and then attempt to respond to it, as that would be unfair to the person who sent the message. Try not to assume anything about the person who posted the message.

◈ When replying to an individual, always be sure that you have copied his e-mail address EXACTLY as it appeared in his original posting. Use the **Copy** and **Paste** trick mentioned on page 33 for foolproof addresses.

◈ If you decide to answer a question from a mailing list, try to determine if the answer you post will be of general interest to all the subscribers. If not, it may be best to answer the question by sending a private e-mail message to the person who posted the original request.

◈ Do not post personal replies or thank-you messages to a mailing list. Send these directly to the person you are thanking.

◆ Other members may send you messages known as *flames* which are meant to express an opposing view or reprimand someone who has done something that is considered inappropriate by other users. To avoid being *flamed*, be sure to check your communications for clear content, spelling and punctuation. Avoid topics and discussions that may be controversial in nature. Do not do any name-calling and do not use any negatively charged words.

◆ Do not send any message to a mailing list on a negative impulse. If you need to respond to something that is upsetting, go ahead and write the message, but set it aside. Look at it again the next day and if you still feel the same way you can send the message if you choose. However, if you send a negative message, be sure you are prepared for a negative response in return.

◆ Remember that with e-mail, it is impossible to read any body language from the person you are corresponding with. So misunderstandings can happen quite easily. Try not to assume anything in your correspondence and work toward clarifying statements before reacting to them.

◆ If you intend to use sarcasm or humor in your messages, be sure to label it clearly as such. Use emoticons or acronyms (see *e-mail* in the glossary) in your message to indicate an emotion in your written message.

◆ Be patient with all "newbies" to a mailing list. Remember that we all started out on the Internet with little knowledge of how things worked. Everyone has to start somewhere!

◆ Keep in mind that the Internet is a global community. You will undoubtedly encounter people from all over the world, so be tolerant of people who do not use English as their native language. Do not use abbreviations or slang terminology on a mailing list, because it may not be something that is understood halfway across the world.

```
┌─────────────────────────────────────────────────────┐
│                    Example                          │
├─────────────────────────────────────────────────────┤
│                                                     │
│  My web site's domain name is www.oz.net, so many   │
│  people assume that I am from Australia because Oz   │
│  is a nickname for that country. Added to that is    │
│  the fact that the abbreviation for Washington State │
│  is WA, which is also the abbreviation for Western   │
│  Australia. This is one example of why abbreviations │
│  shouldn't be used in clear online communications.   │
│                                                     │
└─────────────────────────────────────────────────────┘
```

◈ Never assume anything about other subscribers on the mailing list. Here is one example that illustrates why this is important. One person chastised another subscriber because he asked for someone to look up something in a reference book. This person told the other that if he doesn't own that reference book himself, he should learn to go to a library rather than have others do his research for him. The person who had asked the original favor informed the other that he was unable to do this because of physical disabilities. Don't assume that everyone else on a mailing list can do the same things that you are able to do. Don't assume that they have the same understanding or knowledge on any given topic. When all else fails, give the other subscribers the benefit of the doubt until you have all the facts in any given situation.

Showing Courtesy to Other Subscribers and to Listowners

◈ When someone has replied to something that you posted on a mailing list, be sure to send him or her a thank-you e-mail message. Even a short, one or two sentence reply is better than no reply at all. If you are busy and intend to reply in detail at a later date, just drop the person a quick e-mail explaining what your intentions are.

◈ If you have posted a question on a mailing list, chances are that the other members of the mailing list will now hope to see the answer also. If you receive an answer to that question, be sure to send a message to the mailing list that includes a thank-you to all the people who helped you and also includes the answer to your question. The exchange and sharing of helpful information is what these mailing lists are all about!

◈ Do not post private or personal information about yourself unless you are entirely comfortable with this information becoming public knowledge. Remember everyone's right to privacy and do not post personal information about living relatives on a mailing list.

◈ Remember that all messages to a mailing list will be stored on a server's hard drive and archived for future reference. Each message will take up a bit of valuable storage space while also adding to the burden on the mailing list software program that distributes messages to all the subscribers. Don't post redundant information or replies that have little bearing on the topic. Make sure that your message will be of use to people on the list and that you aren't merely repeating something that has already been discussed. Also keep your messages as short as possible. Do not use your signature file on a mailing list if it contains long lists of surnames. Repetitive posts to a list with these surnames only clutter up the archives. In a search of the archives this will cause a large number of *hits* on the same person who posted the messages over and over again.

◈ Do not send any file attachments to a mailing list. This causes a huge burden on the server and the mailing list software program. It is also considered rude to force a file on people without their consent. Instead, offer your file to the members of the mailing list and send it out individually to those people who are interested in it.

◈ Do not send any junk mail to a mailing list. Do not forward any "warning" messages you receive regarding viruses to a mailing list. Many times these warnings are merely a hoax meant to cause a flood of e-mail. For details, be sure to see *Computer Virus Myths* at **http://www.kumite.com/myths/**.

Research Strategies for Using Mailing Lists

The various genealogy mailing lists are terrific forums for meeting other people who are working on similar lines of research. You will spend much of your time online participating in the discussions that take place on mailing lists. Therefore, you should do everything you can to make your time as productive as possible. The following are a few ideas to help you maximize the potential for mailing list productivity in your online research.

Getting the Most from Mailing Lists

◆ To begin with, take the time to learn about and join the following two mailing lists. These are the best lists to start with online.

1. ROOTS-L
   For broad-based, general genealogical discussions and queries. ROOTS-L is the first genealogy mailing list and it is currently the largest with over 8,000 subscribers to date.

2. GEN-NEWBIE-L
   A mailing list where people who are new to computers and genealogy may interact using a computer's e-mail program. The list discusses genealogy, family history, computer applications and a wide variety of other topics. Members are very tolerant, with a goal of assisting anyone who wants "community coaching" about the Internet, genealogy, computers or whatever.

◆ Also consider joining mailing lists which cover one of your specific areas of research or a surname within your family. Visit either of the two web sites shown below for details of the current mailing lists available for online genealogical research.

◆ **Genealogy Resources on the Internet - Mailing Lists**
http://users.aol.com/johnf14246/gen_mail.html

◆ **Cyndi's List of Genealogy Sites on the Internet - Newsgroups & Mailing Lists**
http://www.oz.net/~cyndihow/newsmail.htm

◆ Learn all you can about your e-mail software program and its various features. Utilize every option in the best manner possible in order to maximize the potential of this very powerful tool.

◆ Use your e-mail program's **Find** feature to do a search through long incoming mailing list messages and digests. Search for surnames, place names or other keywords or topics.

◈ Create a separate mailbox for each mailing list to which you subscribe. Transfer all incoming and outgoing e-mail for each list into the appropriate box for long-term storage and reference.

◈ The genealogy mailing lists are all free to subscribe to and they are meant to be interactive forums. So make them work for you! Don't just sit around and wait for other people to post messages and hope that the right thing makes it into your e-mail **In** box. Post your queries regularly, perhaps monthly. Post your surnames of interest regularly. Every once in a while, make mention of where you are concentrating your research. Let everyone know what your own specialty is, so that they can ask you for advice and help. Make offers of help to the list and consider swapping research services with someone. Use a calendar or workbook and keep track of what days you posted certain information and to what list you posted it. Remember that the membership on a mailing list is never stagnant, but constantly growing and changing. So someone who just joined the list didn't get to see the query you posted last month. That is why frequent postings are so important. Be sure to space them far enough apart so that you aren't being a nuisance, but don't miss the opportunity to share with new members either.

◈ Give a mailing list a fair chance to prove useful. Some lists are very low in traffic and many people get discouraged by this and unsubscribe soon after they first join. Many times there are lulls in conversation on a mailing list and then suddenly the conversation will take off like a rocket! Hang around on a list for a while before you decide to quit. You never know what might pop up!

Queries

◈ Write up a basic query for each person or surname that you are working on. Keep these queries in a document on your computer that is handy at all times. One suggestion is to keep these in a blank e-mail message with no address in the **To:** field. You can keep this e-mail message in your **Out** box indefinitely and use it as a quick place to store and retrieve notes of this type. Whenever you need to send out your query to a mailing list, you can do a quick **Copy** and **Paste** to copy the pre-written query and paste it into a new outgoing e-mail message.

◈ Use the trick described above to write up brief outlines of certain family lines. For example, Family Tree Maker is genealogy software that allows you to copy an Outline Descendant Tree, which you can then paste into an outgoing e-mail message. I use this trick whenever someone contacts me about one of my family lines. But instead of opening up FTM over and over again, I have copied each outline once and keep them in a handy e-mail message in my **Out** box. Then to reply to an incoming inquiry, I just do a quick **Copy** and **Paste** into a new outgoing message. Many times the inquiries I receive are somewhat vague and don't indicate whether there is reason to think we have a connection in our research. So I have found that sending a brief outline with my information saves a lot of back-and-forth messages to try to determine whether we should be corresponding. Following is an example of a brief outline:

```
Descendants of Martin Thomas


1      Martin Thomas
       +Mrs. Sarah Thomas
        b: Unknown in Virginia
       2      John William Thomas
                 b: 1813 in Orange Co, Virginia
                 d: 22 April 1897
              +Mrs. Frances Ann Thomas
                 b: About 1826 in Virginia
                 d: About 1867 in Virginia
                 3      Elizabeth M. Thomas
                           b: 11 November 1853 in Albemarle Co, Virginia
                 3      Henrietta Florence Thomas
                           b: 25 December 1856 in Green Co, Virginia
                 3      Sarah Francis Thomas
                           b: 25 December 1856
                 3      {Girl} Thomas
                           b: 1859
                 3      John W. Thomas
                           b: About 1865 in Virginia
                 3      Benjamin Franklin Thomas
                           b: 20 September 1864 in Nortonsville,
                           Albemarle Co, Virginia
       *2nd Wife of John William Thomas:
       +Mary Ann Leamon
                 b: 31 August 1832 in Virginia
                 3      Samuel Lee Thomas
                           b: June 1871 in Virginia
                 3      Lewis E. Thomas
                           b: About 1873 in Virginia
                 3      Mary E. Thomas
                           b: About 1877 in Virginia
```

❖ As long as you are posting your query or outline to a mailing list, consider using the **Cc:** field in your e-mail message and send a copy to a few other appropriate mailing lists at the same time. Always send one to ROOTS-L, then be sure to send a copy to the mailing list for the locality to which your query pertains and also to a surname list if there is one available for the surnames in your query. **Copy** and **Paste** the query on the *USGenWeb* web site for the county to which your query relates. Again, make this computer software work for you. Use the **Cc:** field, the **Copy** and **Paste** function and other timesaving methods to get the most out of each thing you post!

Searching Techniques

❖ To quickly search a posting from a mailing list, use your e-mail program's **Find** feature. In most programs it will be under the **Edit, Find** menu. Type in a keyword or phrase and press **Enter**. For example, you can use this technique for finding specific surnames, topics or localities. In the instance where you receive your subscription in digest mode, using the **Find** feature is a two-step process. First, it will find a keyword in the index of the digest. Then, to find the specific message within the digest, just choose **Edit, Find, Find Again** (or **Find Next**).

❖ If you are busy or in a hurry, read the subject lines of the messages first. If they don't interest you, you can always use the delete feature. This is why clear and concise subject lines can be so important. If you receive your mailing list postings in digest form, scan the index at the top of the digest if there is one.

❖ Whenever you want to find a message from a previous date, check to see if the mailing list of interest has an archive of past messages. Quite often they do and you can search them from a web site or even order copies via an e-mail message. The ROOTS-L mailing list has its searchable archives online. This includes all messages since its inception in 1987:

> ❖ **Search the Archive of ROOTS-L messages from 1987 through present**
> http://searches.rootsweb.com/roots-l.search.html

◈ You may often find that you get tired of a certain mailing list due to the people who are subscribed or because of a lack of the type of content you were hoping for, etc. If this happens, remember that it is very easy to unsubscribe from the list for a while. You can always re-subscribe and pick it up again when you are ready. That is the beauty of the mailing lists being free and so easy to join!

Examples of Mailing Lists and Newsgroups Currently Available

There is really only one complete online resource for mailing lists and newsgroups:

◈ **Genealogy Resources on the Internet**
http://users.aol.com/johnf14246/internet.html

This terrific web site is faithfully maintained by John Fuller and Christine Gaunt and is divided into individual sections for each component of the Internet: mailing lists, newsgroups, the web, e-mail, FTP, Telnet and Gopher. Visit the *Genealogy Resources on the Internet* web site and you will find all the details you need in order to join and participate in a large variety of genealogy mailing lists. The section of their site which is dedicated to mailing lists is located at **http://users.aol.com/johnf14246/gen_mail.html** and is further subdivided into these categories:

> *General Mailing Lists*
> *Geographic/Non-USA Mailing Lists*
> *Geographic/USA Mailing Lists*
> *Software Mailing Lists*
> *Surname Mailing Lists*
> > **(See the alphabetical table at the bottom of the main index page)**

```
╤╤ Netscape - [Genealogy Resources on the Internet]                    _ |8| X
File  Edit  View  Go  Bookmarks  Options  Directory  Window  Help

  Back  Forward  Home      Edit      Reload  Images   Open    Print    Find    Stop

   Location: http://users.aol.com/johnf14246/gen_mail.html                         N
```

GENEALOGY RESOURCES ON THE INTERNET

MAILING LISTS

URL: http://members.aol.com/johnf14246/gen_mail.html

Last update: July 15, 1997 by John Fuller, johnf14246@aol.com

Usenet Newsgroups | Ftp Sites | Telnet Sites | Gopher Sites | Web and other sites | Email Sites | Text Version(3/19/97) |
Register Resource

Welcome packages are generally provided when you subscribe. It is recommended that these be kept on file since they contain
important information about posting, unsubscribing, and other aspects of list membership that will be useful to you in the future.
Please note that a number of lists are included for various countries and areas of the world where the list descriptions do not

```
 ⌐ Document: Done                                                            ⋈ ?
```

On *Cyndi's List* you will find a category titled "Newsgroups & Mailing Lists." In this category I have attempted to categorize the available mailing lists in a variety of ways that are familiar to all genealogists. Most of the links in these sub-categories lead to specific sections and locations on Fuller's and Gaunt's *Genealogy Resources* web site. Due to John and Christine's hard work, you can be assured that the details for subscribing, unsubscribing and posting to these mailing lists are always current and can be found in the same format and in the same places on their extremely reliable site.

Following is a list of mailing lists and newsgroups that are currently available, as indexed on *Cyndi's List*. All of the mailing list descriptions shown below are courtesy of John Fuller and Christine Gaunt. To obtain current information on how to subscribe, unsubscribe and participate in these forums, go directly to the *Genealogy Resources* web site at **http://users.aol.com/johnf14246/gen_mail.html** or visit the "Newsgroups & Mailing Lists" category on *Cyndi's List* at **http://www.oz.net/~cyndihow/sites.htm** and follow the links!

The First Mailing Lists to Start with Online

◈ **GEN-NEWBIE-L Mailing List**
A mailing list where people who are new to computers and genealogy may interact using a computer's e-mail program.

◈ **ROOTS-L Mailing List**
The original mailing list for genealogy! Broad-based genealogy topics - over 8,000 subscribers.

Military

◈ **AMERICAN-REVOLUTION Mailing List**
For the discussion of events during the American Revolution and genealogical matters related to the American Revolution. The French-Indian Wars and the War of 1812 are also suitable topics for discussion.

◈ **CIVIL-WAR Mailing List**

◈ **WW20-ROOTS-L Mailing List**
For the discussion of genealogy in all 20th-century wars.

Miscellaneous

◈ **ADOPTEES Mailing List**
For legal adoptees and "adoptee-lites" (people who were raised without one or both birth parents, but who were never legally adopted) to seek advice in conducting a search.

◈ **ADOPTING Mailing List**
For anyone touched by adoption. This list offers search help, support and tips on research related to adoption.

◈ **ADOPTION Mailing List**
Discussions of anything and everything connected with adoption.

◈ **CEMETERY Mailing List**
For people interested in the many aspects of family graves, from caring for the grave of one ancestor to the restoration and preservation of the family cemetery.

◈ **CLA-L: Cemetery Listing Association Mailing List**
The purpose of the CLA is to collect cemetery research by

individual genealogists and make it available across the Internet.

◈ **EMIGRATION-SHIPS Mailing List**
A mailing list for anyone who wants to discuss the ships their ancestors arrived on or post passenger lists for any ships.

◈ **GEN-IRC Mailing List**
For Internet Relay Chat.

◈ **GENEALIB Mailing List**
For librarians who specialize in genealogy.

◈ **GEN-EDITOR Mailing List**
For editors/publishers of genealogical, surname and family newsletters to have a place to discuss and share ideas and tips.

◈ **GEN-MARKET Mailing List**
Gatewayed with the soc.genealogy.marketplace newsgroup for commercial postings of unique interest to genealogists.

◈ **GEN-MAT-REQUEST Mailing List**
This is a mailing list for anyone who has an interest in the buying or selling of new or used genealogical materials (e.g., books, newsletters, CDs, magazines).

◈ **GEN-MAT-15-REQUEST Mailing List**
For anyone who desires to post the availability of new or used genealogical materials (e.g., books, newsletters, CDs, magazines) or services for sale at a price of $15 or less.

◈ **GEN-MEDIEVAL Mailing List**
Gatewayed with the soc.genealogy.medieval newsgroup for genealogy and family history discussion among people researching individuals living during medieval times.

◈ **GENMTD-L Mailing List**
Gatewayed with the soc.genealogy.methods newsgroup for the discussion of genealogy research techniques and resources.

◈ **GENMSC-L Mailing List**
Gatewayed with the soc.genealogy.misc newsgroup for general genealogical discussions that don't fit within one of the other soc.genealogy.* newsgroups.

◈ **GEN-OBIT Mailing List**
For obituaries.

◈ **GENTEEN-L Mailing List**
For teenagers and young adults who are interested in genealogical research or others who have suggestions or ideas for young genealogists.

◈ **HOMESPUN Mailing List**
A mailing list for the sharing of homespun tales and genealogy trivia. Postings include a range of topics, such as "Old Sayings," "Old Family Recipes," "Interesting Excerpts from Bibles, Wills, Court Records," "Family Anecdotes," "Folk Medicine -- Cures/Remedies," etc.

◇ **IMMI-GRAND Mailing List**
For those attempting to do genealogical research whose grandparents (or parents) arrived in the U.S. after 1875.

◇ **INSCRIPTIONS-L Mailing List**
For anyone who has an interest in genealogy and local history related to Monumental Inscriptions including gravestones, monuments and war memorials.

◇ **MAYFLOWER Mailing List**
A mailing list for the discussion and sharing of information regarding the descendants of the *Mayflower* passengers in any place and at any time.

◇ **MOUNTAIN-RECIPES Mailing List**
A mailing list for the sharing of down-home country recipes. This list was created as break time for hard-working family historians.

◇ **Photo Generations - Home of the PhotoGen Mailing List Page**
The photography and genealogy mailing list.

Queries and Surnames

◇ **GENNAM-L Mailing List**
Gatewayed with the soc.genealogy.surnames newsgroup for surname queries and tafels.

◇ **RSL-UPDATE Mailing List**
The Roots Surname List database monthly update of new surnames.

◇ **Surname Mailing Lists**
See *Genealogy Resources on the Internet*, http://users.aol.com/johnf14246/gen_mail.html for lists of hundreds of mailing lists for specific surnames.

◇ **SURNAME-QUERY Mailing List**
For users to send queries on specific surname searches.

Religion and Churches

◇ **BRETHREN Mailing List**
Includes such church groups as Tunkers/Dunkers, Church of The Brethren and German Baptists.

◇ **ELIJAH-L Mailing List**
For believing members of The Church of Jesus Christ of Latter-day Saints to discuss their ideas and experiences relating with genealogy in the LDS Church.

◈ **HANDCART Mailing List**
For anyone who has an interest in the genealogy, journals and stories of the Pioneers of The Church of Jesus Christ of Latter-day Saints who settled in the Salt Lake Valley from 1847 to 1860.

◈ **JEWISHGEN Mailing List**
The JewishGen Conference. Discussions of Jewish genealogy. JewishGen is gatewayed with the soc.genealogy.jewish newsgroup.

◈ **MENNO.REC.ROOTS Mailing List**
A Mennonite genealogy and family research interest group.

◈ **MENNO-ROOTS Mailing List**
Another list for Mennonite research.

◈ **MORMON-INDEX Mailing List**
Provides a weekly newsletter containing queries about Mormon Internet resources, responses to those queries, announcements of Mormon Internet resources and compilations of resources by subject.

◈ **QUAKER-ROOTS Discussion Group**
For anyone with an interest in their Quaker heritage.

Software and Computers

◈ **BBANNOUNCE-L Mailing list**
Maintained by the Banner Blue Division of Brøderbund Software for product announcements.

◈ **BK Mailing List**
An experience exchange platform for the Brother's Keeper genealogical program.

◈ **BK5forum Mailing List**
For the discussion of the Brother's Keeper genealogy program. The list is for the Scandinavian countries, so please note that the languages for this list are Norwegian, Danish and Swedish.

◈ **BK5-L Mailing List**
A mailing list for the discussion of the Brother's Keeper genealogy program.

◈ **CFT-WIN Mailing List**
Discussion and support for Cumberland Family Software products.

◈ **FAMILY-ORIGIN-USERS Mailing List**

◈ **FTMTECH-L Mailing List**
Maintained by the Banner Blue Division of Brøderbund Software for the discussion of technical issues regarding the Family Tree Maker genealogy program.

◈ **GEDCOM-L Mailing List**
A technical mailing list to discuss the GEDCOM specifications.

◈ **GENCMP-L Mailing list**
Gatewayed with the soc.genealogy.computing newsgroup for the discussion of genealogical computing and net resources.

◈ **GENWEB Mailing List**
Discussions of the implementation of a genealogical information exchange system using the World Wide Web. Not related to *USGenWeb*.

◈ **NEW-GEN-URL Mailing List**
To announce new genealogy web sites.

◈ **PAF Mailing List**
For discussions relating to the Personal Ancestral File program put out by the LDS church.

◈ **ReunionTalk Mailing List**
A list for discussions of Reunion, the family tree software for Macintosh and Windows.

◈ **TMG-L Mailing List**
A mailing list for those interested in The Master Genealogist software program.

Specific Localities and Ethnic Groups

Mailing lists for each of the U.S. states and the Canadian provinces can be found on the corresponding state or province pages on *Cyndi's List* at **http://www.oz.net/~cyndihow/sites.htm**. Look in the "United States" category and the "Canada" category.

◈ **AFRIGENEAS Mailing list**
For African-American genealogy.

◈ **ALSACE-LORRAINE Mailing List**

◈ **ARIA-L Mailing List**
For Australians and New Zealanders who are researching their Italian heritage, culture and ancestry.

◈ **AUSTRIA Mailing List**

◈ **BADEN-WURTTEMBERG Mailing List**
For Baden, Hohenzollern and Wurttemberg.

◈ **BAHAMAS Mailing List**
For anyone with a genealogical interest in the country of the Bahamas.

◈ **BASQUE-L Mailing List**

◈ **BAVARIA Mailing List**
For the kingdom, province and state of Bavaria including the city of Munich.

◈ **BORDER Mailing List**
For anyone interested in genealogy, history, or culture related to the counties which surround the border of Scotland and England.

◈ **BRAZIL Mailing List**
For anyone with genealogical interest in Brazil.

◈ **BUKOVINA-GEN Mailing List**
For those researching their genealogy and family history in Bukovina, a former crownland of the Austrian Empire (a.k.a. Bucovina, Bukowina, Bukovyna or Buchenland), now divided between Romania and Ukraine.

◈ **CANADIAN-ROOTS-L Mailing List**

◈ **CHANNEL-ISLANDS Mailing List**
For anyone with a genealogical interest in the Channel Islands (Jersey and the Bailiwick of Guernsey) which lie off the Normandy coast of France.

◈ **COMUNES_OF_ITALY Mailing List**
For those who are interested in Italian genealogy, culture and all things Italian.

◈ **CORNISH-L Mailing List**
For anyone interested in immigrants from the county of Cornwall, England to the United States.

◈ **DERBYSGEN Mailing List**
For anyone with a genealogical or historical interest in the county of Derbyshire, England.

◈ **DUTCH-COLONIES Mailing List**
For New York and New Jersey colonies, known as New Amsterdam.

◈ **FIANNA Mailing List**
For those who are researching Irish ancestry and history to discuss ways of improving their skills in searching for their Irish ancestors.

◈ **FINNGEN Mailing List**
For Finnish genealogy.

◈ **GENANZ-L Mailing list**
Gatewayed with the soc.genealogy.australia+nz newsgroup for the discussion of Australia and New Zealand genealogy.

◈ **GENBNL-L Mailing List**
Gatewayed with the soc.genealogy.benelux newsgroup for research in the Benelux region (Belgium, the Netherlands and Luxembourg).

◈ **GEN-DE-L Mailing List**
Gatewayed with the soc.genealogy.german newsgroup for the discussion of German genealogy.

◈ **GEN-FF-L Mailing List**
Gatewayed with the fr.rec.genealogie newsgroup for the discussion of Francophone genealogy -- the genealogy of French-speaking people.

◇ **GEN-FR-L Mailing List**
Gatewayed with the soc.genealogy.french newsgroup for the discussion of Francophone genealogy -- the genealogy of French-speaking people.

◇ **GENPOL Mailing List**
For Polish genealogy.

◇ **GEN-SLAVIC Mailing List**
Gatewayed with the soc.genealogy.slavic newsgroup for the discussion of Slavic genealogy.

◇ **GENUKI-L Mailing List**
Gatewayed with the soc.genealogy.uk+ireland newsgroup for the discussion of genealogy and family history in any part of the British Isles.

◇ **GERMAN-AMERICAN Mailing List**
For anyone interested in genealogy related to German immigrants and their families AFTER their arrival in America.

◇ **GERMAN-BOHEMIAN-L Mailing List**
About the culture, genealogy and heritage of the German-speaking people of Bohemia and Moravia, now the Czech Republic.

◇ **GERMAN-KINGDOMS Mailing List**
For anyone with a genealogical interest in the Duchies of Thuringen, Braunschweig, Lippe, Waldeck, Mecklenburg-Schwerin, Mecklenburg-Strelitz.

◇ **GERMANNA COLONIES Mailing List**
For descendants of the Germanna Colonies (i.e., the original German settlements in Virginia under Governor Spotswood; there were three colonies established, the first being in 1714).

◇ **GERMAN-TEXAN Mailing List**
For anyone with a genealogical interest in German and Central European immigrants to Texas, especially Germans in the 19th century.

◇ **GER-RUS: Germans from Russia Electronic Discussion List**
For general discussions of Germans from Russia culture, folklore, etc.

◇ **GER-RUS2 Mailing List**
For genealogy and family research.

◇ **GIBRALTAR Mailing List**
For those with a genealogical interest in Gibraltar, including those who have Gibraltarian families and those who are researching family members who spent some time in Gibraltar working for the British military or other services.

◇ **HANNOVER-L Mailing List**
Genealogy and history which has a connection to the former Kingdom of Hannover.

◇ **HESSE Mailing List**
For the kingdoms, principalities, provinces and state of Hessen (Hesse-Darmstadt, Hesse-Starkenburg, Hesse-Nassau, Waldeck, Rheinhessen) including the city of Frankfurt-A/Main.

◇ **Hungarian American List (HAL)**
A mailing list for those interested in expressing, sharing and exchanging their views, ideas and feelings about

Hungary, Hungarians, Hungarian-Americans and Hungarian culture and genealogy.

◆ **HUNGARY Mailing List**

◆ **INDIAN-ROOTS Mailing List**
For Native Americans.

◆ **INDIA-ROOTS Mailing List**
For those who are researching their ancestry in Colonial India.

◆ **IRELAND Mailing List**

◆ **KOREA Mailing List**

◆ **LANCSGEN Mailing List**
For anyone with a genealogical or historical interest in the county of Lancaster, England.

◆ **LITHUANIA Mailing List**

◆ **LOYALISTS-IN-CANADA Mailing List**
For those with Loyalist ancestors to help one another research their Loyalist history and to post any facts on the subject that they desire. Loyalists are defined as those who left the United States for Canada after the American Revolution for a number of reasons.

◆ **MECKLENBURG-L Mailing List**
Genealogy and history which has a connection to the general area of Mecklenburg.

◆ **MIDMARCH Mailing List**
For anyone with a genealogical or historical interest in the counties of Herefordshire, Shropshire and Worcestershire, England.

◆ **NA-FORUM Mailing List**
For anyone with an interest in North American Indian history and/or their Indian family history.

◆ **NECKAR-L Mailing List**
For anyone with a genealogical interest in the Neckar River Valley region of southwest Germany (the state and old Kingdom of Wurttemberg).

◆ **NORFOLK Genealogy Mailing List**
For anyone with genealogical interests in the county of Norfolk in England. My husband, Mark Howells, is the listowner for this mailing list.

◆ **NO-SLEKT Mailing List**
Norwegian genealogy conference covering any topic in genealogy except computer programs for genealogical use and searches for lost relatives and ancestors. The conference is conducted in Norwegian.

◆ **NO-SLEKT-ETTERLYSNING Mailing List**
Norwegian genealogy conference for searching relatives and ancestors in Norway and eventual discussions of such searches if there are dubious links published.

◆ **NOTTSGEN Mailing List**
For anyone with a genealogical or historical interest in Nottingham County, England.

◆ **OLDENBURG-L Mailing List**
For those interested in sharing and exchanging information on genealogy and history that has a connection to the former Grand Duchy of Oldenburg.

◈ **OVERLAND-TRAILS Mailing List**
Discussions concerning the history,
preservation and promotion of the
Oregon, California, Sante Fe and
other historic trails in the western
U.S.

◈ **OW-PREUSSEN-L Mailing List**
Genealogy and history which has a
connection to the former East and
West Prussia.

◈ **PENNA-DUTCH Mailing List**
For anyone who is researching their
Pennsylvania Dutch ancestry or has
other genealogical or historical
interests in the Pennsylvania Dutch.

◈ **PIE Mailing List**
For Italian genealogical research.

◈ **POLAND-ROOTS Mailing List**

◈ **POLSKA Mailing List**
For those researching genealogy
related to persons of Polish descent.

◈ **POMMERN-L Mailing List**
Genealogy and history which has a
connection to Pommerania, both the
current Polish part and remaining
German parts of the former Prussian
province.

◈ **PORTUGAL Mailing List**

◈ **PRUSSIA-ROOTS Mailing List**
For anyone with a genealogical
interest in Brandenburg, Hannover
(or Hanover), Ostpreussen (East
Prussia), Pommern (Pomerania),
Posen, Provinz Sachsen (Province of
Saxony - northern Saxony),
Schleswig-Holstein, Schlesien
(Silesia), Westpreussen (West

Prussia), Lubeck, Hamburg and
Bremen.

◈ **SACHSEN-ANHALT-L Mailing List**
Genealogy and history which has a
connection to the present area of the
state of Sachsen-Anhalt.

◈ **SANTA-FE-TRAIL Mailing List**
For sharing ideas, adventures,
questions and answers regarding the
Santa Fe Trail. While not specifically
oriented toward genealogical queries,
other subscribers may be able to
assist you in researching your
ancestors who traveled along this trail.

◈ **SARDINIA Mailing List**

◈ **SLOVAK-L Mailing List**

◈ **SLOVAK-WORLD Mailing List**

◈ **SOUTH-AM-EMI Mailing List**
A mailing list for the discussion and
sharing of information regarding
emigrants from the United Kingdom to
South America during the 18th and
19th centuries.

◈ **SWEDES Mailing List**

◈ **SWITZERLAND Mailing List**

◈ **TRIER-ROOTS Mailing List**
For anyone with a genealogical
interest in Luxembourg, the Saarland,
the Rheinland, Westfalen (Westphalia)
and the Pfalz (used to be between
Rheinland and Baden, belonged to
Bavaria but is now part of Rheinpfalz).

◈ **WESSEX-PLUS Mailing List**
For anyone who has an interest in
genealogy or general and local history

related to the counties of Berkshire, Dorset, Gloucestershire, Hampshire, Oxfordshire, Somerset and Wiltshire, England.

◈ **WESTFALEN-L Mailing List**
Genealogy and history which has a connection to the general area of Westphalia.

◈ **WILTSHIRE-EMI Mailing List**
Regarding emigrants from Wiltshire County, England to anywhere in the world in any time frame.

◈ **YORKSGEN Mailing List**
For research in Yorkshire, England.

Newsgroups

"Gatewayed with" means that a mailing list mirrors the associated newsgroup. All e-mail postings seen on the newsgroup will also be seen on the mailing list and vice-versa. This means that if you have a preference between the two formats, you can choose the one that you like best. Here are some examples of the currently available newsgroups for genealogical and historical research and discussion:

◈ **alt.adoption**
For adoptees, birthparents, adoptive parents.

◈ **alt.genealogy**
General discussion.

◈ **alt.obituaries**

◈ **alt.scottish.clans**

◈ **alt.war.civil.usa**

◈ **fr.rec.genealogie**
Mostly in French. Gatewayed with the GEN-FF-L Mailing List.

◈ **no.slekt**
Mostly in Norwegian. Gatewayed with the NO-SLEKT Mailing List.

◈ **no.slekt.programmer**
Mostly in Norwegian. Gatewayed with the NO-SLEKT-PROGRAMMER Mailing List.

◈ **rec.heraldry**

◈ **soc.adoption.adoptees**

◈ **soc.genealogy.african**
Gatewayed with Afrigeneas Mailing List.

◈ **soc.genealogy.australia+nz**
For Australia and New Zealand.
Gatewayed with GENANZ-L
Mailing List.

◈ **soc.genealogy.benelux**
For Belgium, Netherlands and
Luxembourg. Gatewayed with
GENBNL-L M

Chapter IV

The World Wide Web

The World Wide Web - "The Web"

The World Wide Web, the latest addition to the Internet, has created a wonderful new universe for genealogical researchers. The web is a graphical, multimedia presentation of pages of information on the Internet that can be connected together with *hypertext links*, making an interlocking "web" of sites which are easily reached and navigated. For example, you can start at a web site in California, then follow and click your way through various links, ending up at a web site in Germany. Web pages can include text, pictures, sound, movies, animations, searchable databases, interactive forms to fill out and more.

The possibilities for genealogical research tools that you can find on a web site are almost endless. There are online searchable databases of GEDCOM files, obituaries or cemeteries and even some census indexes and records available. There are military regimental histories, rosters of specific companies or units of soldiers and many other military and history sites of interest. You can learn about specific locality resources by visiting the home pages of genealogical and historical societies, archives, libraries, cities, counties and state governments. Imagine being able to plan a research trip ahead of time to save yourself wasted time once you get to your destination.

There are many interactive, searchable sites that allow you to put in a keyword, topic or surname and perform various functions. For example, there is a site called *Switchboard*, **http://www.switchboard.com/**, which is an online telephone and address directory for the United States. There are also tools such as a Soundex converter, **http://searches.rootsweb.com/cgi-bin/Genea/soundex.sh**, date and calendar conversion sites and search engines for finding web sites and other Internet resources with surnames or place names that you are researching. There are many online tutorials, as well as guides and articles about specific genealogical topics, such as beginning your genealogical research, using census records, using land records or how to use the LDS Family History Library in Salt Lake City. It is like having an entire library of genealogical how-to books at your fingertips, any time day or night!

Many companies are putting their products online with catalogs, samples, demos and special offers. So it is possible to do some of your shopping, or at least do some comparison shopping, for genealogical supplies, books, maps, microfilm and software online. Everton's even has an online version of their *Genealogical Helper* magazine, **http://www.everton.com/b1.htm**, which differs from their printed version. If you've ever had problems hunting down that elusive book or map, you will love being able to track it down easily from the comfort of your own home.

Every day I find several new personal home pages that are being created by people all over the world. There is software available that allows people to convert their GEDCOM files into HTML format, the language of the web. When you find a web page developed with this software, each of the surnames will appear as a clickable hypertext link. This link leads to an index which takes you further to the specific information about that person. Personal home pages quite often will include family pictures and personal family stories too. These pages can be a lot of fun to explore. After you have been surfing the "genealogical net" for a while, you may want to consider putting your own home page up in order to share your genealogy with others, post your personal queries and have a great amount of exposure to other genealogists, thus making possible connections. Just imagine having dozens of researchers, from anywhere in the world, looking at your research and surnames of interest every day!

The Tools You Will Need for the Web

There are three essential components that you will need to have in order to begin using the web:

1. A connection to the Internet via an ISP or commercial online service.

2. A dialer software application for your computer. Windows 95 comes with a dialer resident in the program. Windows 3.1x users need a TCP/IP stack package such as the shareware program, Trumpet Winsock. Macintosh users need MacTCP and MacPPP. These programs come with more recent versions of the Mac operating system software.

3. A web browser software program such as Netscape Navigator or Microsoft Internet Explorer. The commercial online services such as

AOL, Prodigy and CompuServe all come with a web browser resident within their program. See Chapter VI for more web site addresses with software and shareware programs like these.

Getting to Know Your Browser

To visit web sites, you will need a browser. This is a software program designed to access web sites, as well as Gopher and FTP (file transfer protocol) sites. Many times browsers will be able to launch add-on features or programs for other Internet applications such as Telnet, newsgroups and e-mail. There are many browsers on the market now, most of them currently available for download from the Internet. The one that is most popular and well known is the Netscape Navigator. Microsoft also has their own Internet Explorer browser, which is offered as a free download. See Chapter VI for more web site addresses with software and shareware programs like these.

The Netscape Navigator web browser toolbar.

The Microsoft Internet Explorer web browser toolbar.

The following is a list, with descriptions, of some of the toolbar and menu options for a typical web browser:

Back

The **Back** button will take your browser back to the web page you visited just prior to accessing the page you are currently on. You will also find the **Back** option under the **Go** menu.

Forward

The **Forward** button will take your browser forward to a web page that you have visited, assuming you have used the back button already. You will also find the **Forward** option under the **Go** menu.

Example

Using the **Back** *and* **Forward** *buttons is a lot like turning the pages in a book. Starting with the page you are on, you can move backwards or forwards sequentially, based on the sites you have already accessed and the order in which you accessed them.*

Home

The **Home** button will take your browser back to whatever page you have configured as your default preference. This is quicker than using the **Back** button, especially if you have been to multiple web sites and would like to skip revisiting them. You will also find the **Home** option under the **Go** menu. In Microsoft Internet Explorer, this is called a **Start Page**.

Reload

Use this feature to reload a web page in your browser. You would need to reload a page if you had problems loading any part of it, such as the graphics, or if you wanted to be sure that you had the most current version of a web page, rather than relying on the cached version. This option is also available under the **View** menu. In Microsoft Internet Explorer, this is called the **Refresh** button.

Images

One of the menu options available is to turn off graphics or images while visiting web sites. This means that you can visit a web site without the benefit of seeing the pictures and decor chosen by the author. The speed at which the site loads into your web browser is much faster with this option. If you are using this option, the **Images** button on the toolbar allows you to load images for any web page you visit at any time. So if you are curious and just have to see what you might be missing you can use the Images button to load the page again, but this time with graphics in place. You can also load images under the menu option, **View, Load Images**. To turn graphics off in Netscape, go to **Options** and un-check **Auto Load Images**. In Microsoft Internet Explorer, this choice is under the **View, Options** menu.

Open

Press the **Open** button and you are presented with a small window that displays a choice for **Open** or **Open Location**. You can type in the address for a web site that you would like to visit and off you go! You can also do this using the **File** menu option.

Print

You can print any web pages that you are interested in. So if you aren't fond of reading long text documents on your computer monitor, you can print the document and read it offline. There is a **Print** button and also a menu option under **File, Print**.

Find

Use the **Find** button or **Edit, Find** menu feature to search a large site. Enter a keyword you are interested in such as a surname, place or topic. This is particularly helpful if you are visiting a site with a very large index of surnames. This means that you don't have to strain your eyes scanning the monitor for a name to pop out at you - let the browser do the work for you! You can utilize the **Find** function under the **Edit** menu.

Stop

The **Stop** button can be used whenever you would like to stop a web page from loading in your browser. You might use this if you attempt to access a web site, but get no response. Often when this happens, your browser is tied up waiting for the web site to reply. So it is best to use the **Stop** button and then try to access that site at a later time. You will also find the **Stop** option under the **Go** menu in Netscape and under the **View** menu in Microsoft IE.

◈ File

The **File** menu allows you to perform several functions including **New Web Browser** or **New Window, Open Location, Save As** and **Print**.

With the first option, you can open several new web browsers to run simultaneously while you are surfing. This is only limited by your computer's available memory (*RAM*) and by the specified number of browsers in your browser's options menu. Usually opening up to four web browsers all at once is enough, without slowing down the response time too much. This would be helpful when you are visiting a site that you don't want to leave quite yet, but you still feel like taking a little side trip to another web site. Or you could open two web browsers and visit two sites that you would like to compare, side by side · for instance, a site with a map of Virginia counties next to a site with family information from Virginia. Open both web browsers, then drag the sides of the two windows with your mouse and cursor to size the windows so that they fit next to each other on the screen.

The **Save As** feature allows you to "save" the current page onto your computer's hard drive or a floppy disk in order to keep it long-term or to view it later, offline. This is particularly handy for people who have limited amounts of time to spend online, because of expense or because they don't want to tie up their phone line. Just remember that the links on the page won't work unless you are online. So this practice only works best for documents that you wish to read or study. Save the file with a .htm extension. To view it later, open up your browser, choose **File, Open File** and supply it with the directory name and the file name on your hard drive or floppy disk. Your browser will display the file without the need to be online.

◈ Edit

The **Edit** menu allows you to perform several functions including **Cut**, **Copy**, **Paste** and **Find**. The **Find** feature is discussed above. The **Copy** and **Paste** functions are especially important for you to familiarize yourself with. Whenever possible, use this to copy e-mail addresses, web site addresses and mailing list subscription commands to ensure foolproof results.

◈ Go

This feature will show you a menu or history folder of the most recent sites you visited during the current online session. So if you wish to go back several pages, you can skip some of them by using **Go** to find the web site that you wish to revisit. You will also find the **Back**, **Forward**, **Home** and **Stop** (for Netscape) options here.

◈ Bookmarks or Favorites

Bookmarks are a browser feature that allow you to keep track of the web sites you have visited and go back to them later without having to remember or retype the URLs (addresses). In Microsoft Internet Explorer these are called *Favorites*. Once you find a site that you want to bookmark, go to the **Bookmarks** menu and choose **Add a Bookmark**. To return to a site that you already have a bookmark for, go to the **Bookmarks** menu, view the bookmark list and click or double-click on the name of the bookmark. Your browser will attempt to access that site. As you collect many bookmarks, you may want to organize and categorize them to make them easier to use. Read your browser's manual or online documentation to learn how to arrange your bookmarks into folders and a hierarchical organizational system.

◈ Options

The **Options** menu has several features that allow you to set up and customize your web browser. Generally, you will only access this when you first set up your Internet account, then periodically as you learn more about the web and what your own personal preferences are. In Microsoft Internet Explorer, the **Options** choice is under the **View** menu.

◈ Help

Use the **Help** menu whenever you have a question about how your browser works.

How to Access a Web Site

The first thing to do is dial-up your Internet connection, then *minimize* your dialer in the background. You will use your web browser to access web sites. There are several ways that you can access web sites, including these options:

A Home Page or Start Page

Most browsers allow you to pre-configure them so you can access a specific web site each time you start up the program. This is known as your Home Page or Start Page. In Netscape this feature is under **Options, General Preferences, Appearance**. In Microsoft Internet Explorer this feature is under **View, Options, Navigation**. Type out or copy and paste the full URL for the site you wish to use as your default, then click OK. For instance, if you wanted to use my web site as your default home or start page you would type in:

http://www.oz.net/~cyndihow/sites.htm

Typing a URL

You can manually type the URL (address) for a web site into your browser. Use the **Open** button or menu option, and when the **Open** window appears, fill in the URL for the web site. You can type in the URL or use the copy and paste function. Another option is to go to the **Location** box or **Address** box at the top of the browser. This appears just under the button toolbar and is a long, open field with a drop-down menu showing the previous places that have been visited. The URL for the web sites you visit will appear in this field. You can delete the previous entry and type in a complete URL, including all characters exactly as they are shown to you. Or to be safe you can use the fool-proof method of copy and paste to insert the URL in this field. After you enter the URL in the box, press **Enter**. The browser will send messages to your ISP's server and attempt to access that web site. Many URLs are case sensitive, so if you have one that appears in all lower-case letters or a mixture of letters, copy it exactly as you see it. Do not assume that something should be in capital letters because it is a name or proper noun. A computer reads these addresses and the computer is very literal in its thinking. It can distinguish between an upper-case *H* and a lower-case *h*.

```
┌─────────────────────────────────────────────────┐
│                  Helpful Hint                   │
├─────────────────────────────────────────────────┤
│                                                 │
│  Whenever you find a URL in an e-mail message   │
│  or any other type of computer document...      │
```

Helpful Hint
Whenever you find a URL in an e-mail message or any other type of computer document, rather than type it into your browser by hand, try this shortcut. Highlight the full URL with your mouse. To do this, place the cursor in front of the first character you wish to copy. Click the mouse button and drag it across the text to just after the last character you wish to copy. Release the mouse button. Choose **Edit, Copy,** *then toggle over to your open browser window. Place your cursor in the location or address box near the top of the browser and choose* **Edit, Paste.** *By doing this, you can copy the URL exactly as shown and you don't have to be bothered with typing long strings of numbers and letters.*

Following a Link

On a web page you will find many examples of *hypertext links*. Hypertext links are usually a different color from the rest of the text on the page and they are generally underlined. This is done so that they really stand out on the page and catch the visitor's eye. When you place your cursor over one of these links, you will see it change from an arrow to a little hand with a pointing finger. This is like a signal to you that you can click on that spot with your mouse and move to another web page if you like. Click on the link and your browser will send a request to your ISP's server to locate the web site indicated by the link's title.

Moving Around a Web Site

When you type in a URL or click on a link, you will see brief messages at the bottom of your browser that indicate the actions that the browser is taking. For example, you will see messages like "contact host," "host contacted," "waiting for a reply," "3K of 400K loaded" or "10% of 100 loaded." When the connection is completed, the note at the bottom of the browser will say "Document: Done." It is always best to wait until you receive the "Document: Done" message before you start clicking on links and moving to new pages. That way, when you use the **Back** button and return to this page, things will load very quickly.

As the above messages are being shown at the bottom of the browser, you will also see the new web page gradually being loaded into your browser. Many times pictures and graphics are loaded slowly, one line at a time, while text and backgrounds are loaded more quickly. If you aren't interested in the pictures, it is possible to scroll through the page while the document is still loading. You aren't obliged to wait for the pictures. Another option you have in order to speed things up is to turn the graphics feature off. In Netscape, go to **Options** and un-check **Auto Load Images**. In Microsoft Internet Explorer, this choice is under the **View, Options** menu. Now every page you visit will display only its text. If you reach a site that looks interesting and you wish to see the graphics, you can click on the **Images** button in Netscape and reload that page with the graphics and pictures in place. You just have to remember to go back and turn off the graphics again when you are finished. Turning the graphics feature off can save time and memory resources (RAM) on your computer, so it may be

---

the best solution for slower modems or computers with small amounts of memory.

Once a web page is completely loaded you will find many elements to explore. A good web page will have a clear title and stated purpose. The name and e-mail address for the author should also be prominently displayed on the site. Many times there is also a date showing the last revision of the web page. You can use the date to make note of sites that you intend to visit often. If the date changes, you know you might want to spend time looking through the site to see what is new. Web page authors are as unique and creative as any other author or artist, so the variety of web sites will take you from one end of the spectrum to the other. Some web pages will be filled with graphics and pictures. Others will get straight to business and contain a lot of text. A well-designed web page will have an easy plan for navigating throughout the site. This might include an index or table of contents near the beginning. It should also include indicators and links that make it clear as to what you will find once you move to the new location. Each site you visit is as individual as the author, so have fun exploring!

When you click on links that take you to new web pages, then decide that you wish to go back to the previous page, just use your browser's **Back** button. You can back up through each and every page that you have visited. Therefore, if you get lost somewhere on the web, it is very easy to find your way home following the little virtual bread crumbs you left behind! There is also a **Forward** button to use the same way - but in reverse.

If you click on a link and the web site appears to have a problem connecting or is too slow to load, just click on your browser's **Stop** button to interrupt the load. You may want to try once more to access that site, but if you still have problems, just try a different site. Many times there are problems accessing a site if the server at the other end is *down* or if there is too much *noise* or *traffic* on the phone lines and other intermediary connections to the Internet. In my experience, I have learned it is best to go back and try a site a few hours later or even the next day, and I usually don't have any more problems.

The Fancy Stuff: Frames and Plug-ins

There are many web sites out there now that have a lot of new and exciting applications. The possibilities and new features on the web are seemingly endless. It is a challenge just to keep up with the new things you

---

may run across each day. There are animated graphics and icons. There are movies and sound files that you can watch and listen to. There are interactive sites with online quizzes, puzzles and contests. There are web sites divided into windows called *frames*. You can navigate through one frame on a web site, while the other open frames stay the same. To move back in a frame to a previous screen you can use the **Back** button on the browser. In some cases you can also use the right mouse button, which will display a pop-up menu that allows you to navigate with frames.

For many of the new web browser features, you may need to find some add-on applications on the Internet and download them. Examples are Real Audio for audio files and Quick Time for movie files. Many web pages will tell you if you need one of these applications and they even point you to the download sites. These are really fun toys if you have the time to figure out how to use them and if you have the available space on your hard drive to install and store them. However, for everyday genealogical surfing, you most likely won't need them. I haven't yet run across a site that required the use of a plug-in application in order to access the genealogical materials. If you are shown an alert message that tells you to get a certain browser plug-in, you have the option to cancel the alert and continue surfing on that web site. You just won't be able to hear the music or see the movie that the author of the web site placed there. After you become a savvy surfer, you should certainly look into setting up your browser with all the necessary plug-ins so that you can take full advantage of the multimedia facets of the web.

Following are some of the more common browser plug-ins, available for download from these web sites:

◈ **Browsers.com**
   http://www.browsers.com/

◈ **BrowserWatch - Plug-In Plaza**
   http://browserwatch.iworld.com/plug-in.html

◈ **Crescendo**
   http://www.liveupdate.com/crescendo.html

◈ **Download Netscape Navigator Components**
   http://home.netscape.com/try/comprod/mirror/navcomponents_download.html

◈ **Quicktime**
   http://quicktime.atg.apple.com/qthome.html

◆ **RealAudio and RealVideo**
http://www.realaudio.com/

◆ **Shockwave**
http://www.macromedia.com/

Helpful Hint

Be aware that web sites with a lot of animation or a large volume of graphics may hinder your computer's resources. So if you have a small amount of RAM available to you, don't leave your browser on one of these sites for long. If you do, you may have to boot your computer and start up your online session from the beginning.

Surfing - More than Just Web Sites

Once you visit a web site, you will quickly find out why this *surfing* can be so fun and so addictive! You could be visiting a site that is located in Washington state, click on a link to a site in Germany and, once there, click on a link to another site back in New York. After a while, you will see why they call this a "web," as it is based on the pages which are linked together, almost endlessly.

Web pages can have a variety of link types on them. Slowly move your cursor over the link you are interested in. At the bottom of your browser window the URL or address will appear, giving you an idea of the type of site to which this link will lead. If it begins with **http://** you know it is another web site. If it begins with **ftp://** you know it will be accessing an FTP (file transfer protocol) site, which means you may be given options to download a file of some sort.

E-mail addresses can be set up as links as well. The address would start with **mailto:** followed by the e-mail address for the person whose web site you are visiting. If you use Netscape for your e-mail, you can click on this link and a new e-mail message will be launched. If you use a stand-alone e-mail program such as Eudora, you can install a utility that will allow a new e-mail message to be launched in Eudora when you click on an e-mail link in the browser. A web site may also contain links to Telnet systems, Gopher sites and newsgroups. Configure your browser's options

---

to launch a Telnet application for you. Then, when you click on a Telnet link, the Telnet software will run and you will immediately be accessing the Telnet system indicated by the link. Click on a link to a newsgroup and your newsreader will open and access the newsgroup as long as it has been configured properly in your browser.

Tools for Finding Web Sites of Interest

There are several different tools or methods you can use in order to find web sites that may be useful to you in your research, including these four ideas:

1. Search Engines
See *Research Strategies for Using the Web* later in this chapter for more on using search engines.

◈ **AltaVista**
http://www.altavista.digital.com/

◈ **DejaNews** (for newsgroup posts)
http://www.dejanews.com/

◈ **HotBot**
http://www.hotbot.com/

◈ **InfoSeek Ultra**
http://ultra.infoseek.com/

◈ **Lycos**
http://www.lycos.com/

◈ **Web Crawler**
http://webcrawler.com/

◈ **WhoWhere?** (for e-mail addresses)
http://www.whowhere.com/

◈ **Yahoo!**
http://www.yahoo.com/

2. Links List
The easiest way to find web sites is by using a links list, sometimes called a *hotlist*. These are web sites you visit which have lists of links to more web sites. You can benefit from the hard work of others by visiting these already existing lists of genealogy links and begin your genealogical surfing from there. Some links lists are organized and some aren't. Some lists are for specific genealogical topics and some have a variety of links that personally interest the author of that web site. I have found some really interesting sites as I've looked through other user's hotlists. There are several lists of this type online, including my own web site:

◆ **Cyndi's List of Genealogy Sites on the Internet**
http://www.oz.net/~cyndihow/sites.htm

◆ **ROOTS-L Resources:**
United States Resources
http://www.rootsweb.com/roots-l/usa.html

◆ **Genealogy Resources on the Internet**
http://users.aol.com/johnf14246/internet.html

◆ **Searchable Genealogy Links**
http://128.100.201.33/html/lo2.htm

3. From a Friend

Find out about web sites by word-of-mouth from friends and acquaintances or by reading magazines, newspapers, radio and TV.

4. By Surfing

The most fun method for finding web sites is to go online and just start surfing! Start with one web page, click on a link and follow it wherever it may lead you. As you go along, be sure to bookmark sites that you want to visit again. Before long, you will have worked your way around the globe several times and you may be pleasantly surprised by the variety of things that are available online.

Tips and Techniques for Web Surfing Success

◆ Be sure to bookmark sites that you really like and want to return to. See "Research Strategies for Using the Web" in the following section for more on using bookmarks or favorites.

◆ Configure your browser so that all the options are set to your liking. Familiarize yourself with all the buttons and menus. Taking a little time to do this early on will make using the browser that much easier while you are surfing.

◆ Take some time to become familiar with your favorite search engines.

Read the help menus and try a variety of search types to learn the ropes. Use the advanced searching features available on most sites that allow you to tighten the parameters of the search you are performing so that you will get better results. See "Research Strategies for Using the Web" in the following section for more on using search engines.

❖ If you are impatient or in a hurry, turn the graphics feature off on your browser. The web pages will load much more quickly without the graphics in place.

❖ Be sure to dig through a web site and try most of the links to additional pages. Many times I have uncovered beautiful gems of information that were buried several layers deep and were not obvious from the front page or home page on the site.

❖ Learn the keyboard shortcuts for copy, paste and toggling back and forth between applications. This will make things quick and easy when, for instance, you are reading an e-mail or mailing list posting and then want to visit a web site that is mentioned. Using this time-saving method, you can copy a URL from an e-mail message, toggle over to your browser, visit the site, then toggle back to your e-mail program to pick up where you left off. It is very quick and efficient.

For Windows users:

Ctrl + C	=	Copy
Ctrl + V	=	Paste
Alt + Tab	=	Toggles between open applications

For Macintosh users:

| Apple-C | = | Copy |
| Apple-V | = | Paste |

❖ Open more than one web browser window in order to view two or more web sites at the same time. Do this if you want to compare two web pages for similar content. For instance, put a county outline map next to an online history of a particular family and follow their movement within a state. The possibilities of using more than one browser at a time are endless! To open extra browser windows, go to the **File** menu option. Once the extra browser is opened you can toggle back and forth between them or you can size them to fit next to one another.

❖ Use your browser's **Find** or **Search** feature to search web pages for surnames, place names or other keywords. This is especially handy when you find a page with hundreds of surnames listed in an index.

Research Strategies for Using the Web

The following ideas are outlined in as much detail as possible, without referring often to individual features that are specific to certain types of software or certain web sites. In order to make the most of these ideas, it is highly recommended that you learn all that you can about your own personal software programs or about the web sites referenced below. Each program or web site is different and has a different set of instructions to follow. Read the manuals, help files and any web site FAQs that are available. Learning how to use your online tools effectively will increase your chances of finding much more information in a shorter amount of time spent online. Make these online genealogical tools work for you and take advantage of all their wonderful features!

Bookmarks or Favorites

◈ As stated earlier, bookmarks are browser software features that allow you to store the URL or address for a site on the Internet. You can then use the bookmark in order to revisit that site again in the future. By using a bookmark, you can recall the site quickly without having to memorize or type out a long, complicated URL. Some browser programs will also allow you to categorize your bookmarks into folders or directories.

◈ The Netscape Navigator browser creates a new file on your computer called **bookmark.htm**. Each time you add a bookmark or reorganize the existing bookmarks, you are updating this file. It resides in the same directory on your hard drive in which the main Netscape program file is located. You can access this bookmark file in at least three different ways:

1. On the menu bar at the top of the browser, go to **Bookmarks**. When you click on this menu option you will see a drop-down menu which displays the names of the sites that are at the top of your list of organized bookmarks. Therefore, when arranging your bookmarks in a certain order, be sure to put the bookmarks that you use the most at the top of your list for easy access. Use the **Divider** option to put logical spaces between various sections.

Bookmarks - bookmark.htm

File   Edit   Item

```
's Bookmarks
    Cyndi's List of Genealogy Sites on the Internet
    Cyndi's Genealogy Home Page Construction Kit
    Genealogy Resources on the Internet
    Tacoma-Pierce County Genealogical Society
    Tacoma-Pierce County Genealogical Society - Monthly Meetings
    Tacoma-Pierce County Genealogical Society - Activities Calendar
    Tacoma-Pierce County Genealogical Society - PSRoots-L Mailing List
    Tacoma-Pierce County Genealogical Society - Puget Sound Genealogy Resources
    <separator>
    List Owner Utilities for PSRoots Mailing List
    List Owner Utilities for TPCGS-L
    RootsWeb List Owners Utilities Web Pages - Table of Contents
    RootsWeb List Owners - Checklist for Problem Solving
    RootsWeb List Owners - Sample of a Welcome Message to List Users
    RootsWeb List Owners - Samples of Pre-Written E-mail to List Users
    Guidelines for Managing a RootsWeb Mailing List
    RootsWeb - Mailing List Request Form
    <separator>
    AT&T: Wireless Services - Send A Page
    Report Spam E-mail
```

file:///C|/GENEALGY/WEBPAGE/sites.htm

Example of Netscape Bookmarks

2. On the menu bar at the top of the browser, go to Bookmarks. When you click on this menu option, choose **Go to Bookmarks**. A new Bookmark window will open. This is your complete bookmark file and from this window you can click on any name in order to launch the web site address in your browser. In order to organize your bookmarks, highlight a folder or bookmark that you wish to work with and then go to the Item menu option at the top of the bookmark file. There are several options available, including **Insert Folder**, **Insert Separator**, **Insert Bookmark** and **Sort Bookmarks**.

3. Netscape creates bookmarks in a file called **bookmark.htm**. You can view this file using your Netscape browser and each of your bookmarks will appear as hypertext links. To view this file, go to the menu options and choose **File, Open File in Browser**. Choose the directory on your computer where this file is stored. It should be stored in the same directory that your Netscape program is found in. Find the file named **bookmark.htm**, choose it and click on the **Open** button. Your bookmark file will now be displayed just as any other web page would be in your browser. You can highlight the entire file

and directory name in the **Location** box at the top of the browser, then copy and paste this into your web browser options in order to use this as your home page. Each day when you start your browser, your bookmarks will be automatically displayed.

❖ The Microsoft Internet Explorer browser creates shortcuts on your computer to be used as favorites. Each time you add a favorite web site address to the list, a Windows 95 shortcut to that URL is placed in the Windows/Favorites directory on your computer's hard drive. There are two ways to access your favorites:

1. On the menu bar at the top of the browser, go to **Favorites**. When you click on this menu option, you will see a drop-down menu which displays two options followed by the names of the sites that are at the top of your list of organized favorites. Therefore, when arranging your favorites in a certain order, be sure to put the favorites that you use the most at the top of your list for easy access. The two options shown are **Add to Favorites** or **Organize Favorites**. To create a new favorite, use the **Add to Favorites** option when visiting a web site that you would like to access again in the future. Use the **Organize Favorites** option to create folders and arrange your favorites according to your preferences.

2. On the toolbar at the top of the browser, click on the **Favorites** button. When you click on this button you have two choices and a drop-down menu list of your favorites, just as described above.

❖ Arrange your bookmarks or favorites within folders and sub-folders for each of your online interests. For example, you might have a main folder for genealogy. Under that folder you may create several sub-folders for each topic of interest. For example, one for Ohio genealogy, one for England, one for libraries, one for surnames, etc. Under the surname sub-folder you might like to create new folders for each of the surnames you are researching. As you find sites with any of these surnames on them, you can bookmark the site, then store the bookmark in the appropriate surname folder. That way you can return to the site whenever you need to, and your bookmark folder structure will help you find the online resources quickly and easily.

Databases, Personal Home Pages, Surname Lists

◆ Plan a methodical search of the surnames or keywords when visiting any web sites with databases or surname lists that interest you. Keep in mind that web sites are very easy to update, so it is possible for a web site to change, grow and evolve on a daily basis. Check back on each site frequently in order to keep up with additional new information.

◆ Use your browser's **Find** or **Search** feature to search through a transcription or a page of queries for specific surnames that you believe may appear in that county.

◆ Make a note in your research workbook indicating the date that you visited the web page, the name of the web page and the surnames that you searched for on that web page. The next time you visit the page you can check the revision date for that page to see if anything has been added since you last visited the site. If the date has changed, search the page again and make another note in your workbook. Do this for each web site that you visit.

Helpful Hint

Some databases are static and will not increase in size or be updated in any way (i.e., the Pearl Harbor Casualties List). Therefore it isn't necessary to revisit the site unless you need to recheck some of your information.

Hypertext Links

◆ Most web pages have been created with two distinct text colors within a hypertext link. When you first access a web site, the link will appear in one specific color before you click on it. Once you have clicked on the link, it will change to a new color that differs from the original. This is to help indicate to you that the link has been followed or *viewed*. If you use a web site regularly and you want to keep track of which links you have visited, pay attention to the color scheme for the links on that site.

◆ You can set the options in your browser so that the followed or viewed links will remain in the secondary color indefinitely. In doing so, you will be able to work your way through a web site with a long list of links in a methodical and organized manner. As you move through the web page, you will know exactly which links you have already followed. Once you have visited each and every link on a site, you can note in your research workbook that you have completed work on that site on that date. Keeping track of which links you have viewed is particularly helpful when you are working on a certain surname. You may run across a web site that contains a GEDCOM file with clickable links in the records. If this database has thousands of surnames in it, knowing which surnames you have looked at (and which ones you haven't looked at) would be a real timesaver!

◆ You can also set options in your browser so that there are a certain number of days for the link to remain the secondary color, after which it would revert to the original color. If you set this to be for seven days, you could count on the links to be set to original colors once a week. This would be helpful when you have set up a weekly plan to visit specific web sites to check for updates, new queries and additions to the site.

Search Engines

One of the most important tools that you need to familiarize yourself with is the search engine. These are searchable database indexes of resources available on the Internet. A search engine has a software program known as a *robot* that searches the Internet and sets up indexes of the sites that it visits. The robot catalogs the various sites by specific *keywords* with descriptions that help to organize the index. You can use these indexes on web sites and do a search on a word or phrase of your choice, for example "genealogy," "family tree," "maps," etc. The search engine brings back a set of results showing several URLs (addresses) of sites to visit that may match your entry. Each search engine works a bit differently and catalogs site information in a different manner. So try several different engines and also different combinations of words or phrases for maximum search results. There are search engines online that will find web, FTP, Gopher and Telnet addresses, as well as e-mail addresses, mailing lists and newsgroups. The following instructions and ideas are generally similar for all search engines, but be sure to read the online help when you use the search engine web site.

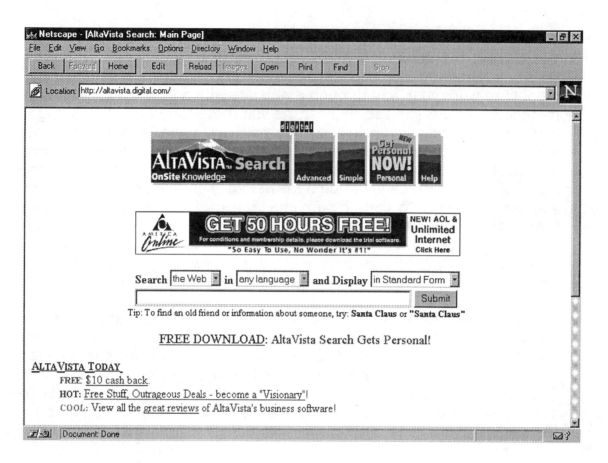

AltaVista is one of the most popular search engine web sites online.

◈ I have found that in using a search engine it is best to begin your search by using broad terms or individual keywords. Don't try to narrow the search with multiple keywords in the first attempt. For instance, if you tried looking for Thomas Jefferson Williams, you might not get any results back. However if you looked for Thomas J. Williams or even just Thomas Williams, you might find that you get several possible matches for your search. You could then look at each match to try and determine whether it contains the topic or information that you are looking for. If you receive too many results and find that none match what you are looking for, you can then begin to tighten the possible results by adding more keywords to the search. Another thought when searching for a person is to remember that some people may use their middle name, rather than their first name. So try searching on J. Williams or Jefferson Williams as well. Perhaps this ancestor uses his initials instead. Therefore, search by using T.J. Williams or just T. Williams as your keywords. Yet another variation might be to search for William Jefferson or William Thomas. With names like these it is very easy for the two names to be in reverse order · either on your own information or in the information contained on another person's web site.

◈ Another example of searching with a constrained set of keywords includes the use of a place name. For example, let's say you search for Thomas Jefferson Williams, Paulding County, Ohio. If you don't receive any satisfying matches here, don't give up! Try changing the person's name as in the examples above, but also take out the county name and use only Ohio. Or take out only the word *county* and see what results you get. Work out as many combinations as possible using this pattern of words to see what results might come back.

◈ **Qualifiers in a Search**

There are several ways to qualify a search in order to specify certain phrases. First, you can group several words together using quotation marks. This will indicate that the search engine should look for a phrase rather than the individual words. Try a search on Ohio Valley Genealogy and you will receive results that include every page (on any web site) that contain the word Ohio, or the word Valley or the word Genealogy. Now try a search on "Ohio Valley Genealogy," including the quotation marks and you should receive results that contain that phrase as shown with the words strung together. Another set of qualifiers to use in this strategy are the + and · symbols. Try this search:

"Ohio Valley Genealogy" ·German +river

and you should receive results for Ohio Valley Genealogy that do not include a German reference, but do include a reference to a river. You can also use the * symbol as a wildcard. For example, search on a partial surname like Thom* and you should get results that include Thomas, Thompson, Thomson and Thomason.

Helpful Hint

The AltaVista and HotBot search engines both make use of the above qualifiers to help you in searching for specific information. Each search engine you try may use qualifiers differently, so read the online help on the search engine web site to learn how to use them for that search engine.

❖ A Boolean Search

Using Boolean logic in a search means incorporating these qualifying terms: *and, or* or *not.* For instance, if you wanted to search on state census records for Rockingham County Virginia, you would phrase your search like this using Boolean logic:

Rockingham **and** Virginia **and** "state census" **not** federal

If there was such a record or reference online, you would receive a set of possible matches back, and they shouldn't contain any note of the federal census. They should also be matches only for Rockingham in Virginia and not any other state. Another example might be appropriate for someone who is researching an ancestor by the name of Boone in Kentucky. Using Boolean logic he could search in this manner:

Boone genealogy **and** Kentucky **not** Daniel

The results should include every Boone in Kentucky, except for Daniel Boone. Keep in mind that this would also exclude all people by the name of Daniel Boone, not just the famous man himself, so there would be no information on any person with that name.

❖ *AltaVista*

http://www.altavista.digital.com/

AltaVista is one of the most powerful search engines online. Its robot scooter automatically finds new sites and notices changes in a web site; then it gathers the information to be indexed. The AltaVista index is updated daily, usually at night. Because the index is constantly changing, you will want to revisit the AltaVista search engine regularly to see what is new. AltaVista uses a ranking algorithm to rank possible matches to your search, with the best match rated highest and listed first in the list of returns. Just under the searchable form on the first page there is a handy tip which gives you hints on how to do searches. This tip is different each time you access the AltaVista web page, so check it often to learn the secrets to making this search engine work for you! Go to the Help link and the Advanced searches link in the graphics at the top of the page in order to learn how to maximize your search options. The AltaVista Advanced searches page is located at http://www.altavista.digital.com/cgi-bin/query?pg=aq.

❖ *Deja News*

http://www.dejanews.com/

Deja News is a search engine that searches through Usenet newsgroup posts for specific names and topics. You can read messages dated at least two months old. Once you find a message of interest, you can also follow the thread by clicking on the subject line link at the top of the page. If you follow the link for the author of the message, you will be able to find other messages posted by that person in other groups and on other topics. You can use Deja News to post new messages and replies to messages without the need for a newsreader. For best results see the *New Users* page and also see the *Power Search* page at **http://www.dejanews.com/forms/dnq.html**.

◆ *HotBot*
http://www.hotbot.com/

HotBot is one of the newest search engines online. It returns by far some of the best matches for the searches that you have it perform. This has quickly become my favorite search engine and the one that I use most often. HotBot's robot, "Slurp," continuously crawls the web looking for new or changed documents. When it finds one, it scans every word on a web site and stores that information in the database. This is what is distinctive about HotBot and why it can give such good results in a search. Many other search engines catalog just the title and/or the first few words or first paragraph on a site. To learn how to make HotBot work its magic for you, see *An Introduction to Using HotBot* at **http://www.hotbot.com/Help/intro.html**.

◆ *WhoWhere?*
http://www.whowhere.com/

WhoWhere? searches the web for e-mail addresses, mailing addresses and phone numbers, individuals or companies and also for web site addresses. Type in the name of a person and you will receive a set of matching results. Follow the individual links further and you will get all the details on that person that are stored in the *WhoWhere?* database. This search engine and others like it are very helpful in finding those long-lost cousins that you have been searching for all these years! See their help page at **http://www.whowhere.com/help/faq.html** for answers to questions about using this database.

◆ *Yahoo!*
http://www.yahoo.com/

Yahoo! is a searchable, hierarchical index of Internet resources, divided and cross-referenced by subject. When you search the *Yahoo!* index, you receive three types of information to fit your request. You will receive the names of *Yahoo!* categories that match your request, you will receive names and links to web sites that match your request and you will receive the name of the *Yahoo!* category under which those web sites are listed. So you can go directly to the web site or you can browse through the *Yahoo!* category to see what types of related sites are also available. To customize your *Yahoo!* search, go to their search options link near the top of the main page. The URL for the search options page is **http://search.yahoo.com/bin/search/options**.

The USGenWeb Project

The *USGenWeb* project is a volunteer effort on a grand scale. It is just a year old and had its start in Kentucky. The idea is that genealogists online volunteer to "adopt" a state and create a web site for that state under the *USGenWeb* project banner. Once the state page is put online, that volunteer then asks for more genealogists to volunteer and adopt a county, then create a web site for that county under the state project banner. Currently every state has a host and over half of the 3,000+ counties in the United States have hosts as well.

County pages for the *USGenWeb* project contain a wide variety of resources for online genealogical research. Each page is as individual as the volunteer who hosts the site. All county pages contain a place for queries regarding research in that county. Anyone can submit a query to be included on the web page. The queries are put on the web site so that anyone can read them. Each *USGenWeb* county page has a set of links that relate to research in that area and lead to other online resources. Some county pages contain lists of addresses for genealogical research facilities in that county, including libraries, archives, museums and societies. A few county pages also contain actual transcriptions of records such as census indexes and records, cemetery listings, ships' passenger lists and more. *USGenWeb* has two terrific projects in the works: the archives and the census project. The aim is to gather transcriptions of source material and store them in one central location, accessible via a corresponding *USGenWeb* county page. All *USGenWeb* pages are clearly marked as belonging to the project and each contains a link back to their corresponding state page and to the main *USGenWeb* page also.

To visit a *USGenWeb* county page, go to the main project home page at **http://www.usgenweb.com/** or visit the U.S. state pages on *Cyndi's List*. Following are ideas for getting the most out of the *USGenWeb* project in your online genealogical research:

◈ Plan a methodical search of the queries on a USGenWeb county page (or pages) that interests you. Keep in mind that web sites are very easy to update, so it is possible for a web site to change, grow and evolve on a daily basis. Check back on each site frequently in order to keep up with what new information has been added.

◈ Use your web browser's **Find** or **Search** feature to search through a transcription or a page of queries for specific surnames that you believe may appear in that county.

◈ Make a note in your research workbook indicating the date that you visited the county page, the name of the county page and the surnames that you searched for on that county page. The next time you visit the page you can check the revision date of that page to see if anything has been added since you last visited the site. If the date has changed, search the page again and make another note in your workbook. Do this for each county that you visit.

◈ Visit the *USGenWeb* archives page for each state and/or county you are interested in. Make a note in your workbook indicating the date you visited the site. Follow the same plan as shown above for queries and revisit a site with archived files at least once a month, making note of the dates on which you visit.

◈ When searching a *USGenWeb* county page, be sure to check the web pages for the surrounding counties as well. To determine which counties are adjacent to the county you are interested in, check a county outline map such as those available from the US Census web site, **http://www.census.gov/datamap/www/**. Many county boundaries changed over time and many of our ancestors paid no attention to county boundaries anyway! If you are looking for ancestors in a specific county, consider the possibility that they lived in any of the surrounding counties during their lifetime.

◈ When posting a query to a *USGenWeb* page, use the **Copy** and **Paste** feature to send a copy of the same query to a mailing list for that county or state. This would also work wonderfully in reverse. When posting a query to a mailing list, copy and paste the query on the corresponding *USGenWeb* county or state page. This way you are getting twice the exposure for your query without much extra effort.

◈ Whenever possible, you might consider adding some of your own resources to a *USGenWeb* county page. If you have source materials available and you want to share them with others, contact the coordinator of the *USGenWeb* county page by e-mail. Let him or her know what you have and that you would like to add your information to the web site. Make sure that your materials are not under a copyright of any sort before you send them to the county coordinator.

◆ If you are adventurous and have time available, you may want to consider adopting an available county and maintain the web site. You don't have to live in the county in order to host the page. Many of the current volunteers don't live anywhere near the actual county that they are hosting. Usually, they have a research interest in that county, so they volunteer to host the page for that reason.

Your Research Workbook

Most researchers keep a workbook that details all of their research efforts to date for each of the ancestors or families that they are working on. Now that you are researching on the web, you are using it as a tool much like you use the library, your Family History Center, genealogical society, or archives. Therefore you should consider adding a new worksheet or a new section to your research workbook in order to keep track of the lines of research you have followed while online.

On a worksheet, include several columns or lines for each of these important source details:

◆ The web site title.
◆ The web site address.
◆ Date of the last revision on the web site.
◆ Date you visited the web site.
◆ Surnames you were researching while visiting the web site.
◆ Other topics you were researching while visiting the web site.
◆ Comments.
◆ Ideas for future visits to this web site.

Helpful Hint

Set up your worksheet as an open document on your computer - either a basic word processing document or a spreadsheet. Have it open in the background while you are surfing. When you need to make a research note, just toggle to your document, type in your notes, then toggle back to your browser and continue surfing!

Examples of Web Sites Currently Available for Genealogical Research

Think of any topic for genealogy and you will be able to find a web site that relates to that topic. Following are just a few examples of available web sites that will assist you with your online research. This list only represents a small sampling of web sites (along with a few Gopher sites) that you will find as you work toward "netting" your ancestors. The addresses were current at the time of the printing of this book; however, with the ever-changing world of the Internet, I cannot guarantee that the addresses will remain unchanged. Many web site URLs in this section are shown on more than one line. However, be sure to type each address as one continuous line of characters when you enter them into your browser.

Cyndi's List of Genealogy Sites on the Internet

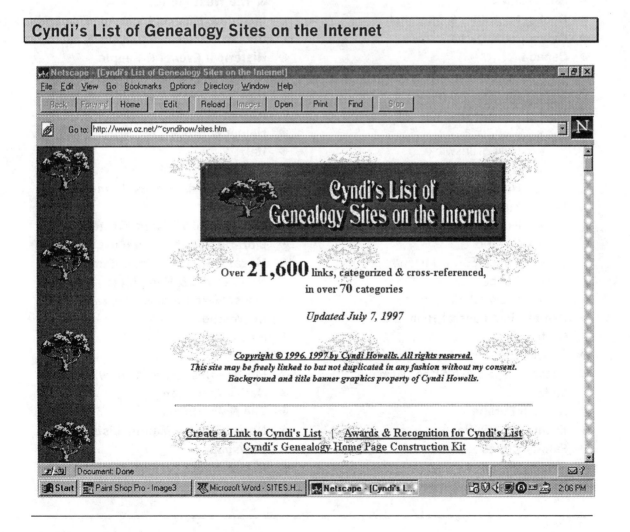

I created my web site so that everyone online could use it as their own personal set of genealogy bookmarks. There are over 70 different categories on over 220 separate pages. All the links are categorized, cross-referenced and listed alphabetically by title in each section. I update my site almost daily and make sure to keep all addresses as current as possible. Set up your browser to start each day with my site, so that my list becomes a jumping-off point for you as you research. Following are the categories that are currently available on *Cyndi's List*:

http://www.oz.net/~cyndihow/sites.htm

- ◈ **Acadian, Cajun & Creole**
- ◈ **Adoption**
- ◈ **African-American**
- ◈ **Asia & The Pacific**
- ◈ **Australia & New Zealand**
- ◈ **Austria**
- ◈ **Belgium**
- ◈ **Biographies**
- ◈ **Books, Microfilm & Microfiche**
- ◈ **Calendars & Dates**
- ◈ **Canada**
  - General Canada Sites
  - Alberta
  - British Columbia
  - Manitoba
  - New Brunswick
  - Newfoundland and Labrador
  - Northwest Territories & The Yukon
  - Nova Scotia
  - Ontario
  - Prince Edward Island
  - Quebec
  - Saskatchewan
- ◈ **Cemeteries, Funeral Homes & Obituaries**
- ◈ **Census Related Sites Worldwide**
- ◈ **Databases, Search Sites, Surname Lists**
- ◈ **Eastern Europe**
- ◈ **Events & Activities**
- ◈ **Family Bibles**
- ◈ **Finding People**
  Phone Numbers, E-mail Addresses, Mailing Addresses, Places, Etc.
- ◈ **France**
- ◈ **Germans From Russia**
- ◈ **Germany**
- ◈ **Handy Online Starting Points**
- ◈ **Heraldry**
- ◈ **Hispanic, Central & South America, & The West Indies**
  Including Mexico, Latin America and the Caribbean
- ◈ **Historical Events & People**
- ◈ **Hit a Brick Wall?**
- ◈ **How To**
- ◈ **Huguenot**
- ◈ **Humor & Prose**
- ◈ **Italy**
- ◈ **Jewish**
- ◈ **Land Records, Deeds, Homesteads, Etc.**
- ◈ **LDS & Family History Centers**
- ◈ **Libraries, Archives & Museums**
- ◈ **Magazines, Journals, Columns, Newsletters & Pamphlets**
- ◈ **Maps, Gazetteers & Geographical Information**
- ◈ **Medieval**
- ◈ **Mennonite**
- ◈ **Military Resources Worldwide**
- ◈ **Native American**
- ◈ **The Netherlands**
- ◈ **Newsgroups & Mailing Lists**
- ◈ **Newspapers**
- ◈ **Occupations**
- ◈ **Odds & Ends**

- ◈ Personal Home Pages
- ◈ Photographs & Memories
  Preserving Your Family's Treasures,
  Stories & Genealogical Research
- ◈ Poland
- ◈ Professional Researchers,
  Volunteers & Other Research
  Services
- ◈ Quaker
- ◈ Queries
- ◈ Railroads
- ◈ Recipes, Cookbooks & Family
  Traditions
- ◈ Religion & Churches
- ◈ ROOTS-L & RootsWeb
- ◈ Royalty & Nobility
- ◈ Scandinavia & The Nordic Countries
  - General Scan. & Nordic Sites
  - Denmark
  - Finland
  - Iceland
  - Norway
  - Sweden
- ◈ Search Engines
- ◈ Ships, Passenger Lists &
  Immigration
- ◈ Societies & Groups
- ◈ Software & Computers
- ◈ South Africa

- ◈ Spain, Portugal & The Basques
- ◈ Supplies, Charts, Forms, Etc.
- ◈ Surnames, Family Associations &
  Family Newsletters
- ◈ Switzerland
- ◈ Terms, Phrases, Dictionaries &
  Glossaries
- ◈ United Kingdom & Ireland Index
  - General UK Sites
  - Channel Islands
  - England
  - Ireland & Northern Ireland
  - Isle of Man
  - Scotland
  - Wales
- ◈ United States
  - An individual page for each
    state
  - General U.S. Sites
  - Library of Congress
  - National Archives
  - Social Security
  - Territories & Possessions
  - U.S. - Census
  - U.S. - Civil War ~ War for
    Southern Independence
  - U.S. - Military
- ◈ USGenWeb & WorldGenWeb Projects
- ◈ Western Europe

Libraries and Archives

- ◈ **Allen County Public Library
  Historical Genealogy Dept.**
  http://www.acpl.lib.in.us/
  departments/genealogy.html

- ◈ **Archives of Australia**
  http://www.aa.gov.au/

- ◈ **HYTELNET on the World Wide Web**
  http://moondog.usask.ca/hytelnet/
  An index of library catalogs online,
  with links to the Telnet addresses
  and complete logon instructions.

- ◈ **LDS Family History Centers**
  http://www.genhomepage.com/FHC/
  Addresses and hours of operation in
  the U.S. and around the world.

◈ **The Library of Congress**
http://lcweb.loc.gov/homepage/
lchp.html

◈ **The Library of Virginia**
http://leo.vsla.edu/index.html

◈ **Libweb - Library Servers via WWW**
http://sunsite.berkeley.edu/Libweb/

◈ **Los Angeles Public Library**
History and Genealogy Department
http://www.lapl.org/central/
hihp.html

◈ **NAIL Home Page - NARA Archival Information Locator**
http://www.nara.gov/nara/nail.html
A pilot database of selected holdings
of the U.S. National Archives.

◈ **National Archives and Records Administration (NARA)**
http://www.nara.gov/

◈ **The National Archives of Canada**
http://www.archives.ca/

◈ **The National Archives of Ireland**
http://www.kst.dit.ie/
nat-arch/index.html

◈ **The National Library of Canada**
http://www.nlc-bnc.ca/

◈ **Netlink: Library Catalogs sorted by Geography/Country Codes**
http://honor.uc.wlu.edu/net/
catalogs/Library_Catalogs_sorted
_by_Geography.html

◈ **The Newberry Library**
http://www.newberry.org/

◈ **New York Public Library**
http://www.nypl.org/

◈ **National Union Catalog of Manuscript Collections (NUCMC)**
http://lcweb.loc.gov/coll/nucmc/
nucmc.html
A free-of-charge cooperative
cataloging program operated by the
Library of Congress

◈ **Public Libraries of Europe**
http://dspace.dial.pipex.com/town/
square/ac940/eurolib.html

◈ **Public Record Office of England and Wales**
http://www.open.gov.uk/pro/
prohome.htm

◈ **San Francisco Public Library**
http://sfpl.lib.ca.us/

◈ **Seattle Public Library**
http://www.spl.lib.wa.us/

◈ **State Library Web Listing**
http://www.state.wi.us/agencies/
dpi/www/statelib.html

◈ **Tacoma Public Library**
http://www.tpl.lib.wa.us/

◈ **U.S. Public Libraries on the WWW**
http://www.tiac.net/users/mpl/
public.libraries.html

◈ **webCATS: Library Catalogues on the World Wide Web**
http://library.usask.ca/hywebcat/

Link Lists

◈ **The Genealogy Home Page**
http://www.genhomepage.com/

◈ **Genealogy Resources on the Internet**
http://users.aol.com/
johnf14246/internet.html

◈ **ROOTS-L: United States Resources**
http://www.rootsweb.com/
roots-l/usa.html

◈ **Searchable Genealogy Links**
http://128.100.201.33/html/
lo2.htm

Locality and Ethnic Specific Sites

◈ **The Afrigeneas Homepage**
http://www.msstate.edu/Archives
/History/afrigen/index.html
For African-American genealogy

◈ **Canadian Genealogy and History Links**
http://www.islandnet.com/
~jveinot/cghl/cghl.html

◈ **FEEFHS - Federation of East European Family History Societies**
http://feefhs.org/

◈ **German Genealogy Home Page**
http://www.genealogy.com/
gene/index.html

◈ **Hispanic Genealogy Crossroads**
http://members.aol.com/
mrosado007/crossrds.htm

◈ **The Italian Genealogy Home Page**
http://www.italgen.com/

◈ **JewishGen: The Official Home of Jewish Genealogy**
http://www.jewishgen.org/

◈ **Native American Genealogy**
http://members.aol.com/
bbbenge/front.html

◈ **Palatines to America**
http://www.genealogy.org/
~palam/

◈ **Scandinavian Genealogy Pages**
http://www.algonet.se/
~scandgen/

◈ **UK+Ireland Genealogy - GENUKI**
http://midas.ac.uk/genuki

◈ **The USGenWeb Project**
http://www.usgenweb.com/

There are so many personal home pages online now that it is virtually impossible to find a favorite. About the time that I think I have found my all-time favorite, I will run across a new site that simply floors me! Below are just a few of the web sites that I have visited and that have impressed me. However, please keep in mind that this is by no means a complete list. Visit the Personal Home Pages category on *Cyndi's List* for links to thousands of terrific sites like these!

◈ **Alex Glendinning's Home Page**
http://user.itl.net/~glen/
Alex has a fascinating web site filled with family stories and pedigrees, informative articles on research in the Channel Islands and in Hungary and a really fun feature called *The Family Face*.

◈ **Ancestors From Norway**
http://www.geocities.com/ Heartland/Plains/5100/
Articles and links to other web sites, all arranged with a focus on Americans who are researching their Norwegian ancestry. This is a terrific site from John Føllesdal.

◈ **The Atkinson and Bass Family Tree**
http://users.quicklink.net/ ~atkinson/
A beautifully designed site by Richard Berrie Atkinson, Jr. The old-fashioned look and feel of his site is very appropriate!

◈ **Brenda's Guide To Online Pennsylvania Genealogy**
http://www.geocities.com/ Heartland/Plains/8021/ palinks.htm
An extremely well-organized set of links to Pennsylvania resources on the web, from Brenda Uplinger.

◈ **Chester County Genealogy**
http://www.rootsweb.com/ ~pacheste/chester.htm
Mary Harris has created a great example of the USGenWeb concept! There are details on numerous Chester County, Pennsylvania resources, as well as cemetery transcriptions and ships' lists.

◈ **Donna Speer Ristenbatt Genealogy**
http://www.ristenbatt.com/ genealogy/
Donna's site has resources for Dutch research, Mennonites, Palatines, Loyalists and much more.

◆ **Elizabeth Orsay's Genealogy Web Page**
http://www.iquest.net/~etorsay/genealogy/
Elizabeth not only put her research and surnames online, she also created a wonderful tool for online researchers to use - United States Vital Records Information.

◆ **Family Roots of Pictou County, Nova Scotia**
http://www.rootsweb.com/~pictou/index.htm
Morgan Robertson has packed this site to the brim with ships' passenger lists, cemetery lists, surnames, links, stories and history regarding this area in Canada.

◆ **Family Tree and History of John Jewell**
http://www.dcscomp.com.au/jewell/family-history/
A truly wonderful site by Bruce Jewell of Australia, complete with details, photographs, stories and links to each ancestor's and descendant's information.

◆ **The Gene Pool**
http://www.rootsweb.com/~genepool/
Joanne Rabun's beautiful web site with extensive resources, including The Quaker Corner, Serendipity Story Board, Oregon History and Genealogy Resources, The Ball Room and Horseneck Founders of NJ.

◆ **Genealogy Software Springboard**
http://www.toltbbs.com/~kbasile/software.html
Karen Basile created this terrific site to help researchers determine which software program is best for them to use. All of the major software programs are listed on this site with complete details and a list of pros and cons submitted by actual software users!

◆ **Ian Clapham's Home Page**
http://www.voyager.co.nz/~ianclap/
This New Zealander has created one of the most comprehensive online genealogy resources for research in his country.

◆ **Ohio River Valley Families**
http://www.tbox.com/orvf/
The ORVF Database Project currently contains information on over 16,935 related family members. Owned and maintained by Allen David Distler.

◆ **The Olive Tree Genealogy Homepage**
http://www.rootsweb.com/~ote/
An unending supply of terrific source material as well as helpful guides and articles! Lorine McGinnis Schulze's site includes resources for these topics: New Netherland, New York, Ontario & Loyalists, Mohawk Nation, Mennonites, Palatines, Irish Info, Ships' Lists, Huguenots & Walloons, Militia Rolls and New Jersey.

◈ **Palatine and Pennsylvania Dutch Genealogy**
http://www.geocities.com/
Heartland/3955/index.html
A comprehensive site from Kraig Ruckel, including surname lists, queries, family Bibles and more.

◈ **Thiessens' Index**
http://www.netcom.com/~jog1/
This great web site by Jo Thiessen is packed full of transcriptions from many types of historical documents regarding her personal research. The topics include Kentucky, Mennonites and Germans from Russia. She has pages for wills, cemeteries, estate settlements and other miscellaneous documents.

Research Guides, Tools and References

◈ **20 Ways to Avoid Genealogical Grief**
http://www.rootsweb.com/
roots-l/20ways.html

◈ **Beginner's Guide to Family History Research**
http://biz.ipa.net/arkresearch/
guide.html
By Desmond Walls Allen and Carolyn Earle Billingsley.

◈ **Books We Own**
http://www.rootsweb.com/~bwo/
A list of resources owned or accessed by fellow researchers who are willing to look up genealogical information for you.

◈ **Cyndi's Genealogy Home Page Construction Kit**
http://www.oz.net/~cyndihow/
construc.htm

◈ **Family Tree Maker Online's Genealogy "How To" Guide**
http://www.familytreemaker.com/ma
inmenu.html

◈ **Historical Maps**
http://www.lib.utexas.edu:80/
Libs/PCL/Map_collection/
historical/history_main.html
From The Perry-Castañeda Library Map Collection, The University of Texas at Austin.

◈ **John R. Borchert Map Library**
http://www-map.lib.umn.edu/
At the University of Minnesota. Contains a wonderful list of links to other map libraries online.

◈ **Journal of Online Genealogy**
http://www.onlinegenealogy.com/
This monthly online magazine is full of helpful articles. Be sure to see the columns from past issues also.

◈ **Land Record Reference**
http://www.ultranet.com/~deeds/
landref.htm

◈ **LDS U.S. Research Outlines**
http://hipp.etsu.edu/ftpdir/
genealogy/LDStext/
Online text version of these valuable
guides for each U.S. state.

◈ **National Archives Catalogs of
Microfilm Publications – On the
Genealogy Page**
http://www.nara.gov/publications/
microfilm/
Each of the catalogs for the Federal
Censuses, as well as the Military
Service catalog, Immigrant and
Passenger Arrivals catalog and many
more.

◈ **Researching Ancestors from the
United Kingdom**
http://www.oz.net/~markhow/
uksearch.htm
Using the LDS Family History Center
Resources.

◈ **Salt Lake City Here We Come!**
http://www.rootsweb.com/
~genepool/slc.htm
Tips on making your Salt Lake City
research trip a big success...from
some helpful folks who have been
there!

◈ **Surname to Soundex Code Converter**
http://searches.rootsweb.com/
cgi-bin/Genea/soundex.sh

◈ **United States Vital Records
Information**
http://www.inlink.com/~nomi/
vitalrec/
A list, by state, of addresses and
details necessary for ordering copies
of vital records.

◈ **U.S. Gazetteer from the U.S. Census
Bureau**
http://www.census.gov/
cgi-bin/gazetteer

◈ **Welcome To The Family History
Center™**
http://www.lds.org/
Welcome_to_FamHist/Welcome_to
_FamHist.html
An online brochure from the official
LDS Church web site.

◈ **Yale Peabody Museum: Geographic
Names Information System (GNIS)**
http://www.peabody.yale.edu/
other/gnis/
Over 1.2 million records which
correspond to labeled features on the
topographic maps of the U.S. These
features include churches,
cemeteries, bodies of water and
many more. Search this database by
county, by feature and by keyword.

❖ **The 1801 Census of Norway**
http://www.uib.no/hi/
1801page.html

❖ **1871 Ontario Census**
http://stauffer.queensu.ca/
docsunit/searchc71.html

❖ **Ancestry Home Town**
http://www.ancestry.com/
main.htm
Ancestry has several searchable
databases, including the *Social
Security Death Index* and *Early
American Marriage Records*. They also
offer helpful articles, professional
research help and products for sale.

❖ **BCCFA - The British Columbia
Cemetery Finding Aid**
http://www.islandnet.com/bccfa/
A database of approximately 200,000
interments from more than 2,000
cemeteries in British Columbia,
Canada.

❖ **Canadian Expeditionary Force**
http://www.archives.ca/db/cef/
index.html
An index to the personnel files of over
600,000 soldiers who enlisted during
the First World War.

❖ **Civil War Soldiers and Sailors
System**
http://www.itd.nps.gov/cwss/
A computerized database project by
the National Park Service. Currently
contains over 230,000 names of
soldiers in the U.S. Colored Troops.

❖ **Convicts Transported to Australia**
http://www.ozemail.com.au/
~jsnelson/convict.html

❖ **Family Tree Maker Online**
http://www.familytreemaker.com/
They have searchable databases,
including the Family Finder Index.
This index contains about 123 million
names from census records,
marriage records, Social Security
death records, family trees and more.

❖ **FEEFHS Surname Database Cross-
Index**
http://feefhs.org/index/
indexsur.html
At least 31 surname databases to
search, from the Federation of East
European Family History Societies.

❖ **GENDEX -- WWW Genealogical Index**
http://www.gendex.com/gendex/
An index which contains over
120,000 different surnames and 2.5
million individuals whose data is
found on hundreds of web databases.

❖ **Genealogy's Most Wanted**
http://www.citynet.net/
mostwanted/
A surname registry database for
those elusive ancestors.

❖ **Ghosts of the Klondike Gold Rush**
http://Gold-Rush.org/
Including history, stories, a timeline
and the *Pan for Gold Database* of
people who were in the Yukon during
the Gold Rush.

◆ **Index to Maine Marriages 1892-1966**
http://www.state.me.us/sos/arc/
archives/genealog/marriage.htm

◆ **Miami Valley Ohio Genealogical Index**
http://www.pcdl.lib.oh.us/miami/
miami.htm
An index of census, tax, will and marriage records for these counties in Ohio: Butler, Champaign, Clark, Darke, Greene, Hamilton, Mercer, Miami, Montgomery, Preble, Shelby, Warren.

◆ **OCFA - The Ontario Cemetery Finding Aid**
http://www.islandnet.com/ocfa/
homepage.html
The Ontario Cemetery Finding Aid is a pointer database consisting of the surnames, cemetery name and location of over 2 million interments from more than 3,800 distinct cemeteries, cairns, memorials and cenotaphs in Ontario, Canada.

◆ **Online Genealogical Database Index**
http://www.gentree.com/
An index of links to web sites with searchable genealogical databases.

◆ **Roots Surname List -- Interactive Search**
http://www.rootsweb.com/
rootsweb/searches/rslsearch.html
Over 250,000 surnames in this database which can be searched by surname or by soundex code. Use the online form to submit your surnames as well!

◆ **RootsWeb Search Engines**
http://www.rootsweb.com/
rootsweb/searches/
Includes The Roots Surname List (RSL), The Roots Location List (RLL), the ROOTS-L Archives of past messages to the mailing list and databases for many U.S. states, including Arkansas, California, Louisiana, South Carolina, South Dakota, Tennessee, Vermont and Wisconsin.

◆ **Seventh-day Adventist Periodical Index**
http://143.207.5.3:82/search/
Has a searchable obituary index and more

◆ **State of Illinois Public Domain Land Tract Sales Archive, 1815-1880**
gopher://gopher.uic.edu/11/
library/libdb/landsale

◆ **U.K. Marriage Witness Indexes**
http://midas.ac.uk/genuki/mwi/
Indexes of witnesses to marriages in the United Kingdom, Australia and New Zealand.

◆ **USGenWeb Census Project**
http://www.usgenweb.com/
census/
Established to transcribe Federal and State Census Records to be placed in the USGenWeb archives.

Societies and Groups

◆ **Federation of Genealogical Societies**
http://www.fgs.org/~fgs/

◆ **The National Genealogical Society**
http://www.genealogy.org/~ngs/

◆ **National Society Daughters of the American Revolution**
http://www.chesapeake.net/DAR/

◆ **New England Historic Genealogical Society**
http://www.nehgs.org/

◆ **Society of Australian Genealogists**
http://www.cohsoft.com.au/afhc/sags.html

◆ **Society of Genealogists, UK**
http://www.cs.ncl.ac.uk/genuki/SoG/

◆ **Sons of Confederate Veterans**
http://www.scv.org/index.htm

◆ **Sons of the American Revolution**
http://www.sar.org/

◆ **Sons of Union Veterans of the Civil War**
http://suvcw.org/

◆ **United Daughters of the Confederacy**
http://www.hsv.tis.net/~maxs/UDC/

Vendors - Books, Software, Maps, Supplies, Etc.

◆ **AGLL Genealogical Services**
http://www.agll.com/

◆ **Ancestral Quest for Windows**
http://www.ancquest.com/

◆ **Barbara Green's Used Genealogy Books**
http://www.wavenet.com/~genbooks/

◆ **Corel Family Tree Suite**
http://www.corel.com/products/familytree/familytreesuite/

◆ **DeedMapper Software**
http://www.ultranet.com/~deeds/factsht.htm

◆ **Family Origins - Parsons Technology**
http://www.parsonstech.com/

◆ **Family Tree Maker**
http://www.familytreemaker.com/

◆ **Genealogical Publishing Company**
http://www.genealogical.com/

◆ **The Gold Bug**
http://www.goldbug.com/

◆ **Hearthstone Bookshop**
http://www.hearthstonebooks.com/

◆ **Heritage Books, Inc.**
http://www.heritagebooks.com/

◆ **The Master Genealogist**
http://www.WhollyGenes.com/

◆ **Picton Press**
http://www.midcoast.com/~picton/

◆ **Reunion**
http://www.leisterpro.com/

◆ **Ultimate Family Tree - Palladium Interactive**
http://www.uftree.com/

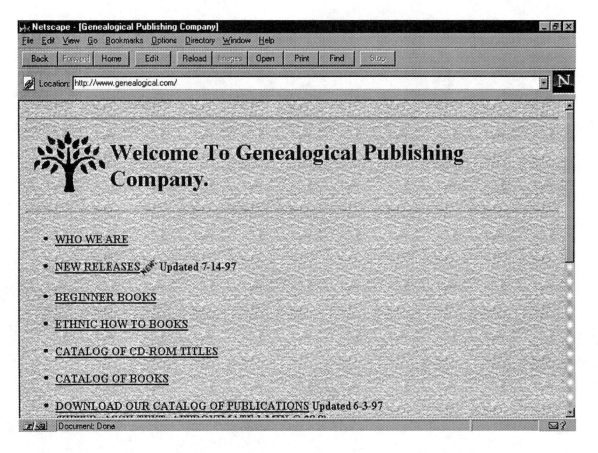

Genealogical Publishing Company has its catalog of publications online.

Chapter V

Other Options for Furthering Your Genealogical Research on the Internet

Other Options for Furthering Your Genealogical Research on the Internet

The majority of this book covered the three most important aspects of genealogical research on the Internet: e-mail, mailing lists and the web. Once you have mastered those areas, you may be interested in exploring some other applications and ideas for researching on the Internet.

IRC - Internet Relay Chat

IRC or Internet Relay Chat is live, real-time text conversations with other Internet users, using an IRC client software program. Once you have dialed-up your internet connection, start your IRC software program and then log onto one of several networks. After connecting with the network, you can join any channel in order to chat with others regarding a specific topic. There are several networks and channels for genealogy, including **#genealogy** and **#genealogy2** on DALnet and **#genealogy** on EfNet. All IRC channels for genealogy can be used free of charge.

◆ **The DALnet Genealogy Channels**
http://www.geocities.com/
Heartland/1486/dalnetgy.html

◆ **Home Page for Genealogy on IRC**
http://www.genealogy.org/
~jkatcmi/genealogy-
irc/welcome.html

◆ **The Unofficial Dalnet and EfNet #genealogy Channels Home Page**
http://ic.net/~goroke/channel.htm

◆ **Ircle IRC Client for Macintosh**
http://www.xs4all.nl/~ircle/

◆ **MacIRC Client for Macintosh**
http://www.macirc.com/

◆ **mIRC IRC Chat Client for Windows**
http://www.mirc.co.uk/

◆ **Pirch Chat Client for Windows**
http://www.bcpl.lib.md.us/
~frappa/pirch.html

Telnet

Telnet is an application that allows you to use your Internet connection and log onto other computers that are connected to the Internet. You then use those remote computers in "real time." When connected to a Telnet site, your computer will look and act as though you were sitting right in front of the computer that you are connected to at the time. Telnet sites can access library catalogs, databases, Archie (see the glossary) and Gopher sites. For example, you can search a library's online card catalog for a specific book or topic via your Telnet connection, without having to visit the actual library itself. Most Telnet sites will tell you to use a specific logon ID and they will have instructions listed for you to follow as you go through each of the menus. Make note of the logon name and password when you begin in case you are asked for it again during your online session. Also make note of the exit instructions when you start your Telnet session. You will need a Telnet software application to access these sites. The software can be configured to launch automatically via your web browser whenever you click on a Telnet hypertext link. Telnet addresses always begin with **Telnet://**.

❖ **HYTELNET on the World Wide Web**
http://moondog.usask.ca/hytelnet/
An index of library catalogs online, with links to Telnet addresses as well as complete logon instructions.

❖ **NCSA Telnet for Macintosh**
ftp://ftp.ncsa.uiuc.edu/Mac/
Telnet/Telnet2.6/

❖ **NetTerm for Windows 95**
http://starbase.neosoft.com/
~zkrr01/

❖ **SJCPL's List of Public Libraries with Telnet Services**
http://sjcpl.lib.in.us/homepage/
PublicLibraries/
PubLibSrvsTelnet.html

A Personal Home Page of Your Own

Once you have been online for a while, you will have seen a large variety of personal home pages. It may now be time to consider putting up a home page of your own. A personal home page for genealogy is like having your own personal billboard on which you can advertise your surnames and research efforts. It is a great way to share information and resources with others also. Make note of the types of things you've seen on other personal home pages. Take the best of those ideas and start to draft out an idea of what you would like to include on your own home page. At the very least, you will want to include a list of the surnames you are working on. At the most, you can put your entire GEDCOM file on the site, along with sources, notes and full details on your research. Consider adding transcriptions, extractions of records and helpful articles. Putting these types of resources on your web site ensures return visitors to your site. I recently created a new web site titled *Cyndi's Genealogy Home Page Construction Kit,* which contains tips, hints, links and more to help you create your personal genealogy home page. It was designed to be a quick start guide to creating and designing a genealogy web page of your own. Creating a web site of your own isn't nearly as hard as you might think. It is a lot of fun, so give it a try · you have nothing to lose and several long-lost ancestors to gain!

◈ **Cyndi's Genealogy Home Page Construction Kit**
http://www.oz.net/~cyndihow/construc.htm

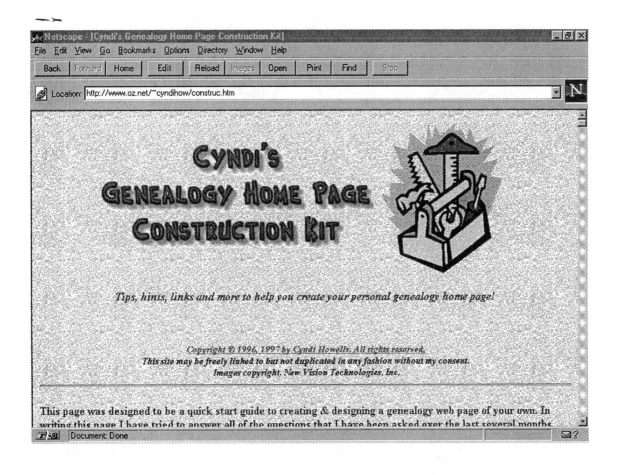

Chapter VI

Downloading Software

FTP / Download Sites
For Software, Utilities and Demos

Use your web browser to visit the sites below and download software, shareware and freeware for use on your own computer. These sites have copies of compression (zipping) programs, virus scanner programs and many Internet applications such as web browsers, newsreaders, e-mail programs, FTP clients and other popular utilities and add-ons. Some of the programs and files on these sites are freeware and some are shareware, so familiarize yourself with the registration requirements for each. After downloading any file from the Internet, you should always be sure to run your virus scanning software. I have created a directory on my computer's hard drive called "Download." Every time I download a file of any sort, I put it in this directory. I regularly run my virus scanning software on this directory to be sure that the files I have downloaded are safe to use before I do anything with them. Keeping all new files in this Download directory also helps me to keep the contents of my hard drive neat and organized.

Popular Software / Shareware Sites

◈ **Macintosh Internet Software Updates**
http://www.tidbits.com/iskm/iskm-soft.html

◈ **NoNags**
http://ded.com/nonags/main.html

◈ **Shareware.com**
http://www.shareware.com/

◈ **Stroud's Consummate Winsock Apps List**
http://cws.wilmington.net/inx.html

◈ **Tucows**
The Ultimate Collection of Winsock Software
http://www.tucows.com/

◈ **The Well Connected Mac**
http://www.macfaq.com

Compression (Zipping) Utilities

◈ **PKWare, Inc., for PKZip Shareware**
http://www.pkware.com/

◈ **Stuffit and Stuffit Expander for Macintosh**
http://www.aladdinsys.com/

◈ **WinZip Home Page**
http://www.winzip.com/winzip_x.htm

◈ **ZipIt for Macintosh**
http://www.awa.com/softlock/zipit/zipit.html

E-mail

◈ **Claris E-mailer**
http://www.claris.com

◈ **Eudora Light and Eudora Pro**
http://www.eudora.com/

◈ **Pegasus Mail**
http://www.pegasus.usa.com/

FTP Clients

◈ **Cute FTP**
http://www.cuteftp.com/

◈ **Fetch Macintosh FTP Client**
http://www.dartmouth.edu/pages/softdev/fetch.html

◈ **FTP Explorer**
http://www.ftpx.com/

◈ **WSFTP for Windows**
http://204.71.8.24:80/junodj/

Genealogy Software Programs

Visit the "Software & Computers" category on *Cyndi's List* **http://www.oz.net/~cyndihow/sites.htm** for a complete and current listing of genealogy software programs, utilities, helpful articles and more.

Miscellaneous

◆ **Cookie Central - Cookie Software Menu - For PC or Macintosh:**
http://www.cookiecentral.com/files.htm
http://www.cookiecentral.com/macfiles.htm

◆ **Internet Starter Kit for Macintosh Internet Resources**
http://www.mcp.com/hayden/iskm/
This book is online and there are links to software and other resources.

Newsreaders

◆ **Anawave Gravity Newsreader for Windows 95/NT**
http://www.anawave.com/

◆ **Free Agent Newsreader for Windows**
http://www.forteinc.com/

◆ **InterNews Newsreader for Macintosh**
http://www.dartmouth.edu/~moonrise/

◆ **Newswatcher for Macintosh**
http://charlotte.acns.nwu.edu/jln/progs.html

Security Programs for Homes with Children

For households with children, there are many software programs on the market that will help you set up certain limits on what type of access you have with your Internet Service Provider. They will help you block out certain questionable Internet sites, and they can also prevent the use of your credit card without your knowledge.

◆ **Cyber Patrol**
http://www.cyberpatrol.com/

◆ **CYBERSitter**
http://www.solidoak.com/

◆ **Net Nanny**
http://www.netnanny.com/home.html

◆ **Surfwatch**
http://www.surfwatch.com/

Virus Scanners

◈ **Disinfectant for Macintosh**
http://charlotte.acns.nwu.edu/
jln/progs.html

◈ **McAfee Virus Scan**
http://www.mcafee.com/

Helpful Hint

Once you are online, be sure to run your virus checking program regularly. Set up a routine to run the program on your computer's hard drive at least once a month. Run the program on all floppy disks that are given to you and be sure to use it to check all new files downloaded from the Internet.

As new computer viruses are introduced daily, the virus signature list resident in your software program needs to be updated in order to be kept current. Many manufacturers of virus scanning programs will offer you updated signature lists via their web sites. I use McAfee Virus Scan on my computer. It runs constantly in the background, runs scheduled disk checks and I update the list of virus signatures frequently as new lists become available. By doing so, I am assured that my computer and its data are protected.

Web Browsers

◈ **CNet's Browsers.com**
http://www.browsers.com/

◈ **Netscape Navigator**
http://home.netscape.com/

◈ **Microsoft Internet Explorer**
http://www.microsoft.com/ie/

Glossary of Internet Terms

Glossary of Internet Terms

For further definitions of Internet terms, visit the following web site:

◈ **Net Lingo: The Internet Language Dictionary**
http://www.netlingo.com

Archie:

A program that functions as a type of index and search tool for FTP (see page 162) sites. Archie programs at different sites may have different indexes of FTP sites and they can be very busy. You use Archie access software or you can Telnet to a site that is running that software. Search engines on the web can also search for FTP sites, so this indexing function isn't as popular anymore.

Bandwidth:

A reference to the amount of capacity available to carry traffic over a typical connection to the Internet. Each phone line, wire, cable or "pipe," which connects you to your ISP and the ISP's server to the Internet backbone, has a limited amount of space available. So information traveling back and forth (in what are called packets) has to take turns when a line is heavily used. People will refer to bandwidth when discussing web pages that are loaded with large graphics, indicating that the webmaster is using too much *bandwidth* by doing so. If a web page takes an inordinate amount of time to load, it is considered that too much bandwidth is being used. Similarly, the frivolous use of quoting back large e-mail messages (unless entirely necessary for the conversation) on a newsgroup or mailing list uses too much bandwidth. If you have an option to download a file from a server close to your location, but choose to download from a server halfway across the world, you will be using bandwidth that could be more efficiently used by someone else.

BinHex:

This stands for BINary HEXidecimal and refers to a method of translating non-ASCII computer files into ASCII or plain text.

Bookmarks or Favorites:

A browser software feature that allows you to store the URL or address for a site on the Internet so that you can revisit that site again later. By using a bookmark, you can recall the site quickly without having to memorize or type out a long, complicated URL. Some browser programs will also allow you to categorize your bookmarks or favorites into folders or directories.

Bounce:

A reference to e-mail that is undeliverable and returns or "bounces" back to the sender.

Browser or Web Browser:

The software that allows you to access and "browse" through WWW, FTP and Gopher sites. Examples of browsers are Netscape Navigator or Microsoft Internet Explorer.

◈ **Microsoft Internet Explorer**
 http://www.microsoft.com/ie/

◈ **Netscape Navigator**
 http://home.netscape.com/

Cache or History:

Whenever you visit a web site, all of the files from that site are temporarily downloaded to your computer's hard drive, sometimes into a directory called *cache* or *history*. The next time you visit a site your browser can recall the documents quicker because they are stored on your computer. If there is an updated version of the site online, some browsers will recognize this and ignore the cached version, loading the updated version instead. When visiting a really important site, if you want to be sure that you get the most recent version just press the **Reload** or **Refresh** button on your web browser's toolbar. Cache has a limited directory size, so the files are rotated through, with the newest files displacing the oldest files. You can set the size of your cache directory by checking the options or preferences menus in your browser.

Cookies:

Cookies are bits of data which are fed or given to your web browser by the web server you are attempting to connect with. Your browser can also return bits of data to the server, but only the data that the browser itself contains (i.e., your name, e-mail address, browser version, etc.). It is not possible for a cookie to retrieve other information from your hard drive outside of what a previous cookie has already put there or the data that the browser already contains (e-mail address, version, etc.). We have yet to see any proof in the media that indicates that cookies are harmful in any way · to you or to your computer.

The data in a cookie file is designed to make return visits to web sites easier, quicker and/or more efficient. Examples of the use of cookies can be found whenever you visit a site which has a "shopping cart." As you plan to buy something online you can add items to the "shopping cart" and move on to another page in the online catalog. There are several online genealogy bookstores or commercial sites which use this type of program. The items you choose are added to your cookie file so that when you are ready to close the transaction and pay for the items all of the information is readily available. Many of the customizable online news services work the same way by using cookies. Following are web sites which explain cookies and their use:

◈ **Cookie Central**
   http://www.cookiecentral.com/

◈ **EPIC's Cookies Page**
   http://www.epic.org/privacy/
   Internet/cookies/

◈ **Malcolm's Guide to Persistent Cookies Resources**
   http://www.emf.net/~mal/
   cookiesinfo.html

Cyberspace:
A reference to the electronic universe of the Internet.

Digest:
An alternate option for mailing list subscriptions. Digests will be made up of several mailing list posts that have been made throughout the day. People who receive a digest rather than individual messages will only get the digest once or twice a day depending on the number of posts to the mailing list. The digest will usually have an index at the top which is made up of the subject lines from each e-mail message contained within the body of the digest.

Download:
The process of receiving e-mail messages or transferring computer files from a server through your Internet connection. Each time you check .for incoming e-mail messages, you are *downloading* those messages from

the e-mail server at your ISP or commercial online service to your own computer. Each time you visit an FTP site or attempt to access files and save them to your computer, you are downloading those files.

E-MAIL - Electronic Mail:

Mail messages that are sent electronically via the Internet to other Internet users or to anyone with an e-mail address that can be reached via the Internet. Using an e-mail address, you send the message through your own Internet connection to another Internet user. You use an e-mail software package to create and send, receive and view, print and store e-mail messages. The following is an online e-mail tutorial:

❖ **Internet Navigator - Communicating Over the Internet**
http://www.lib.utah.edu/navigator/email/email.html

Emoticons - Express an Emotion in E-mail Messages

❖ **Emoticons - or - The Smiley Home Page**
http://www.lib.utah.edu/navigator/email/emoticon.html

❖ **The Unofficial Smiley Dictionary**
http://www.eff.org/papers/eegtti/eeg_286.html

Angel	O:-)	Mad	>:-(
Crying	:'(	My lips are sealed	:-X or :-#
Cutsie smile or clown	:o)	Raspberry	:-P*
Devil	}:>	Rose	@-->-->--
Dunce	<:-)	Smile	:) or :-)
Frown or sad	:-(	Smile with glasses	8-)
Hug	{}	Sticking out tongue	:-P
Laughing or big grin	: D or :-D	Wink	;) or ;-)
Kiss	:-*	Yell	:-O

Acronyms Used in Everyday E-mail Messages

- AFAIK As far as I know
- BAK Back at the keyboard
- <BG> Big grin
- BRB Be right back
- BTW By the way
- FWIW For what it's worth
- FYI For your information
- <G> Grin

- GMTA   Great minds think alike
- IMHO   In my humble opinion
- IMO   In my opinion
- LOL   Laughing out loud
- OTOH   On the other hand
- ROFL   Rolling on the floor laughing
- TIA   Thanks in advance
- TL   'Til later
- TTFN   Ta-ta for now!
- TTYL   Talk to you later
- VBG   Very big grin

FAQ:

Frequently asked questions; pronounced "fack." There are often FAQ files available for most subjects and sites on the Internet, especially mailing lists and newsgroups. A FAQ is the best place to start to find answers to your basic questions.

Fidonet:

A system of passing packets of e-mail messages regarding a certain topic among related bulletin board services that are not a part of the Internet. With the advent of the WWW and the Internet becoming more accessible and more affordable, the future of Fidonet seems unsure. E-mail, mailing lists and newsgroups serve the same function on the Internet.

Flames:

Also *flaming* or being *flamed*. A slang term for e-mail messages sent to someone in order to express an opposing view or to criticize or reprimand another user for what might be considered inappropriate behavior. Being clear, concise, careful and courteous in your messages and postings should help you to avoid being flamed. However, there are always some people out there with differing opinions and outlooks. Many times these people are quick to judge and feel that they have to *flame* someone else. The best defense is to remember not to take any messages like this personally and ignore the person doing the flaming.

Freeware:

Software programs that are free to use and do not require any payment to be made to the owner. Sometimes there are certain restrictions on the use of the program, so read the accompanying documentation for details.

FTP - File Transfer Protocol:

The application on the Internet which allows computer servers to send files to one another. You can access an FTP site with a web browser or with an FTP software client program. Once you have connected with an FTP site, you can select from the list and download files that are stored on that site. Examples of files that you can download are software, data or text files, GEDCOMs, graphics, etc.

GEDCOM:

Stands for GEnealogical Data COMmunication. This is a standard developed by the LDS Family History Department, which allows for people to trade their personal genealogy database files with other people regardless of what software program they use. For example, if you want to give your Family Tree Maker file to someone who uses Reunion, you would export or convert your file into a GEDCOM file with a .ged file extension. When the other person is ready to view your file, he would import your GEDCOM file into his software program and convert it to the Reunion format.

Gopher:

The ancestor to the web without all the pretty pictures! It is a menu-driven system used as an interface to the Internet. You can access all sorts of information including databases, file archives and text documents. Gopher sites on the Internet contain sets of files that are kept in a hierarchical menu system, usually represented as folders or directories. Originally, using Gopher and its access software was a process that would "go for" and gather titles of files on other computers and help you get to the information contained there by *tunneling* through the menu system. With the popularity of the web, many Gopher sites are being converted into or duplicated as web pages now. However, there are still many Gopher sites available. For people who have older computers or slower modems, accessing Gopher sites can be a great alternative to using the web. Because these sites are just straight text, the quicker load time and ease of access is preferred by many people.

Home Page:

Generally the opening page or title page on a web site. A home page should contain the title, the author's name and e-mail address, the date that the site was last updated and an index or set of links which help you explore the remainder of the pages on the web site. It is also a good idea to include a statement which makes the intent of the web site clear.

HTML - Hypertext Markup Language:

The computer programming code or language used to create a simple ASCII text file with various HTML *tags* enclosed in <> brackets. These tags define how to format and display web pages, images, etc. in a web browser.

Internet:

The global network of computer networks. The Internet began with a group of government and university systems connecting together in order to share resources and information. The Internet is held together by a series of connections that all follow one another infinitely around the planet. The backbone is the "skeletal" structure of the Internet. It connects supercomputers in major metropolitan cities all around the globe. Internet Service Providers, universities and other institutions connect to the backbone through high-speed lines, and information that is passed from one group to another is directed on the Internet via the use of a *router*. Your computer or network connects to your ISP via a telephone line. Your computer connects to the telephone line with a *modem*. A household connection to the Internet follows this basic structure:

Your modem and computer ➔ Telephone line ➔ Computer or network at your ISP ➔ Routers ➔ Dedicated, high-speed lines ➔ The Internet backbone.

IRC - Internet Relay Chat:

Live, real-time text conversations with other Internet users, using an IRC client program. Once you have dialed-up your Internet connection and started your IRC software program, you log onto one of several networks. After connecting with the network you can choose a channel to join in order to chat with others regarding a specific topic. There are several networks and channels for genealogy, including #genealogy and #genealogy2 on DALnet and #genealogy on EfNet.

◈ **IRC Intro File for Newbies Using Windows**
http://www.geocities.com/SiliconValley/Park/6000/ircintro.html

ISP - Internet Service Provider:

The company, university or institution that sells you the service that allows you to access their computer/server so that you can connect to the Internet. A commercial service such as America Online, CompuServe or Prodigy is not considered an ISP. However, you can access the Internet through one of these services by using their gateway to the net. See

"Getting a Direct Internet Connection" in Chapter I for details on the best account services to look for when choosing an ISP.

Listowner or List Manager:

The person responsible for day-to-day operations of a mailing list. The listowner makes sure that all commands are successfully handled by the mailing list software and helps users of the list with any problems while subscribing or unsubscribing. The listowner determines the rules and guidelines for the mailing list and writes the welcome messages and FAQs for the list. He also enforces those rules and guidelines whenever necessary and has the final approval when dealing with problems regarding the list.

LISTSERV, SmartList, MAISER, ListProc and Majordomo (For Mailing Lists):

These are mailing list management software programs. They are interactive automated software programs on Internet servers that distribute e-mail to subscribers of mailing lists. These programs allow you to issue commands to them via e-mail. To join or *subscribe* to a mailing list, you send an e-mail message to the computer's address with a specific command in the body of the message. You can also quit or *unsubscribe* from that list in the same manner. Once you have successfully subscribed to a mailing list, the mailing list management software program forwards to you copies of all e-mail messages that are posted to the list by other subscribers. Each program works similarly but has its own specific commands and options. Once you learn about a mailing list you wish to subscribe to, you should familiarize yourself with the commands of the program that runs that list. Usually these commands will be detailed within the welcome message or *FAQ* for that list.

Lurking:

Lurking refers to reading mailing list or newsgroup entries and learning the ins and outs of that group for a little while before you actually join in and begin posting messages yourself. By lurking, you can learn a lot about how mailing lists or newsgroups work, about netiquette and about what types of genealogical researchers are out in cyberspace with you.

Mailing Lists:

These are lists made up of groups of people who are interested in specific topics. Once you subscribe to a list, you will receive e-mail messages from the other subscribers of that list. You can receive individual messages or a *digest* of the messages. The digest is a compilation of several messages that are indexed. As you read through the messages in your list, you can send in replies, opinions, answers or solutions, as you like. When you send in a posting or a reply, it is sent via e-mail to the mailing list. Then everyone who is a subscriber of the list receives a copy. In this manner, every subscriber sees all communication that takes place on the list. When someone posts a message to the list, his or her e-mail address and sometimes a name will also appear. You can also privately communicate with another subscriber, if necessary, without posting to the mailing list in general. An example of a mailing list is ROOTS-L, a broad-based genealogy mailing list with over 8,000 subscribers. There is a web site at:

◈ **ROOTS-L Home Page**
http://www.rootsweb.com/roots-l/roots-l.html

MIME:

Multi-purpose Internet Mail Extensions. The latest standard for e-mail message structures. Using the MIME standard allows for easier transmission of e-mail messages with attachments. Be sure that the options in your e-mail software program are set to send and receive MIME compliant e-mail files.

Modem

The hardware that allows your computer to "talk" to another computer via a telephone line. The word *modem* stands for "modulate" and "demodulate." The information you send from your computer cannot be transmitted over a telephone line until it is *modulated*. Once it arrives at the destination, it must be *demodulated* so that it can be received and processed by the computer there.

Moderator

The moderator is a person or persons who screen all incoming messages on a mailing list or newsgroup. He checks each message to be sure that it fits the group's guidelines and that it is appropriate to be posted to the mailing list or newsgroup.

Netiquette:

Appropriate behavior expected of people who use the Internet. This can involve everything from using appropriate language in your communications, to being considerate of other people's needs and feelings.

Following are a few examples of basic netiquette:

◈ Some people may be charged for incoming e-mail by the number or by the length of the messages that they receive. So netiquette would require that you keep messages short and concise as a courtesy to them. Do not send file attachments with an e-mail message until you have asked the person receiving the file whether they would like it or not.

◈ Newcomers to a mailing list or newsgroup should refer to "welcome" messages and documents known as FAQs (Frequently Asked Questions). By doing so, they can find answers to common questions that have previously been addressed. This is a courtesy to the more experienced members of the mailing list or newsgroup.

◈ Newcomers to a mailing list or newsgroup should also try to get the feel of a list or group for a while before joining in and posting responses or questions. This is known as lurking.

◈ Users should carefully read and even re-read a posting before sending it to the mailing list or newsgroup to be sure of its content and to make certain that the intent behind the posting is clear.

◈ You should also keep to the topic of a specific group or list. Posting something that doesn't belong on that list will only clutter it up and waste time for other members of the group.

◈ Other members may send you messages known as *flames* which are meant to express an opposing view or reprimand someone who has done something that is considered inappropriate by other users. To avoid being *flamed*, be sure to check your communications for clear content, spelling, etc. and avoid topics and discussions that may be controversial in nature.

◈ Be sure that you are conveying your true meaning and, if possible, quote your sources.

◈ Generally, text that is written in all capital letters is regarded as *shouting* at someone and should not be done. The exception to this would be for those of us in genealogy who use all capital letters to show surnames.

◈ **Basic newsgroup and mailing list "Netiquette"**
http://www.herald.co.uk/local_info/genuki/netiquette.html

◈ **The Net: User Guidelines and Netiquette**
http://www.fau.edu/rinaldi/netiquette.html

Netizen

A "net" citizen. This usually refers to people who use common courtesy and follow the general guidelines and netiquette while participating in online activities.

Network

A series of computers connected together to perform a specific function. Many offices contain a computer network so that information can be shared easily between co-workers. The Internet is *THE* worldwide network of computer networks.

Newbie:

Someone that is new to the Internet. It shouldn't be assumed that newbies to the Internet are also newbies to genealogy, although the popularity of the Internet is bringing many brand-new genealogists to the community every day.

Newsgroup:

See Usenet Newsgroups below.

Search Engines:

Web sites that have software programs known as *robots* that search the Internet and set up indexes of the sites that they visit. They catalog the various sites by specific *keywords* that help to organize the index. You use search engines in order to do a search on a word or phrase of your choice, such as "genealogy," "family tree," "Ohio map," "Smith," "vital records," etc. The search engine then seeks this information in its index and gives you back a set of results showing you several URLs or addresses for sites to visit that may match your keyword search. Each search engine works a bit differently from another and they each catalog site information differently. Therefore, try several different search engines and different combinations of words or phrases for maximum search results. Search engines can find WWW, FTP, Gopher and Telnet sites, as well as e-mail addresses, mailing lists and newsgroups. Examples of popular web search engines are:

◈ **AltaVista**
   http://www.altavista.digital.com/

◈ **DejaNews** (for newsgroup posts)
   http://www.dejanews.com/

◈ **HotBot**
   http://www.hotbot.com/

◈ **WebCrawler**
   http://webcrawler.com/

◈ **InfoSeek Ultra**
   http://ultra.infoseek.com/

◈ **WhoWhere?** (for e-mail addresses)
   http://www.whowhere.com/

◈ **Lycos**
   http://www.lycos.com/

◈ **Yahoo!**
   http://www.yahoo.com/

Server:

A host computer used to store, transfer or route information from one Internet location to another. Several servers will make up a network that is connected to the Internet. Your ISP may have several servers, each with a separate function. One may store and deliver your incoming and outgoing e-mail messages. Another may be the server which "serves" up web pages to users on the Internet.

Shareware:

Software programs that can be reviewed on a trial basis. Once your trial period has expired, you must register the software and send payment to the owner of the program in order to continue using it.

Signature, Sig or Sig File:

A small text file that is automatically attached to the end of each outgoing e-mail message that you send. Many e-mail software programs have a function for you to use to create a signature file. Signature files should be simple and kept to about 5 or 6 lines. The length of each line should be no more than 70 characters wide in order to be easily read by a variety of e-mail reader software programs. Signature files can contain a person's name, e-mail address and a home or business address. Some people online even put in their favorite verses or quotes and some artwork. For genealogy research purposes, it is a good idea to use a signature file. Be sure to give your full mailing address in case the person reading the message doesn't have direct e-mail access and wants to contact you by *snail mail*. List the most important surnames you are currently researching, so that other researchers can read through them and make a connection with you. There is a helpful web site regarding signature rules and etiquette at:

◈ **Signature Etiquette and a Signature Collection to View**
   http://www.math.fu-berlin.de/~guckes/elm/elm.sig.etiquette.html

SLIP and PPP:

Serial Line Internet Protocol and Point to Point Protocol. Two protocols which give you dial-up access to the latest features on the Internet. PPP is the preferred protocol, being quicker, more efficient and capable of new features. When you sign up for an Internet account with an ISP, be sure to ask for a PPP account.

Snail Mail:

An Internet user's slang term for regular postal mail.

Spam:

Similar to "junk mail," spam refers to unsolicited copies of e-mail messages that are sent out to multiple e-mail addresses with the idea of forcing the message on e-mail users. Often these messages are cross-posted to several mailing lists and newsgroups all at once. Generally spammed messages are from commercial ventures, many of which may not be entirely legal or ethical.

❖ **Fight Spam on the Internet**
   http://spam.abuse.net/spam/

❖ **Yahoo! - Junk e-mail**
   http://www.yahoo.com/
   Computers_and_Internet/
   Communications_and_Networking
   /Electronic_Mail/Junk_E-mail/

Surfing or Surfin' the 'net:

A slang term for browsing on the web, typified by moving from web site to web site using pre-defined hypertext links.

SYSOP:

System Operator. The person in charge of the daily computer operations for your Internet Service Provider or commercial online service.

TCP/IP - Transmission Control Protocol and Internet Protocol:

The standard protocol or "language" of the Internet. This is the process that computers use to communicate with one another on the Internet by sending packets of information back and forth at very rapid speeds.

Telnet:

Allows you to connect with other computers that are connected to the Internet and use those remote computers in "real time." When connected to a Telnet site, your computer will look and act as though you were sitting right in front of the computer that you are connected to at the time. Telnet sites can access library catalogs, databases, Archie and Gopher sites. For example, you can search a library's online card catalog for a specific book or topic via your Telnet connection, without having to visit the actual library itself. Most Telnet sites will tell you to use a specific logon ID and have instructions listed for you to follow as you go through their menus. Make note of the logon name and password when you begin in case you are asked for it again during your online session. Also make note of the exit instructions when you start your Telnet session. You will need a Telnet software application to access these sites. The software can be configured to launch automatically via your web browser whenever you click on a Telnet hypertext link.

Thread:

A string of ongoing discussions on a certain topic which takes place on a mailing list or in a newsgroup. A user will follow a thread when he reads messages and continues to post inquiries or responses specific to some original posting on a mailing list or newsgroup.

Upload:

The process of sending your computer files and e-mail messages to a server through your Internet connection. Each time you send outgoing e-mail messages you are uploading those messages from your own computer to the e-mail server at your ISP or commercial online service.

URL - Uniform (or Universal) Resource Locator:

The address for an Internet site. For the web or WWW, the URL always starts with **http://** and Gopher, FTP and Telnet addresses each start with **gopher://, ftp://** and **telnet://**. The rest of the URL will include the domain name, also known as an Internet address or DNS (Domain Name System) address. The DNS address is noted in words, showing a breakdown of the hierarchy of that site. You can learn the hierarchy by reading the address in reverse order. The DNS address will end with **.gov** (government), **.com** (commercial businesses), **.org** (non-profit organizations), **.edu** (educational), etc. These extensions are designations used in the United States. Outside the U.S., the DNS addresses end with a two character country code, such as: **.uk** (United Kingdom), **.no** (Norway), **.ie** (Ireland). The following is an example of a DNS address for the commercial software site which is titled "Family Tree Maker Online: Genealogy 'How To' Guide": **http://www.familytreemaker.com/mainmenu.html**. What this DNS address shows us is that it is a commercial site (.com) and its domain name is "familytreemaker.com." The "mainmenu.html" that follows the address is the name of a file kept at that site. It happens to be their main "How To" index page and it is a file written in HTML or *Hypertext Markup Language*. Other examples of file extensions you may see are **.txt** (text file), **.jpg** (graphics file), **.zip** (zipped file) and **.wav** (sound file).

Usenet Newsgroups:

Usenet is a service that hosts over 9,000 newsgroups that cover specific topics. Newsgroups are discussion forums where readers can post articles or e-mail messages relating to the topic for that newsgroup. They can also post responses to the articles or messages and, in turn, read responses posted by others. To access a newsgroup, you use newsreader software that allows you to browse through the article headers, read the articles and post responses or new articles to the various newsgroup "discussions." You may also access some newsgroups using a Gopher site or even a BBS, but it's not as easy or convenient as it is to use a newsreader. Examples of newsgroups are **soc.genealogy.computing** or **soc.genealogy.german**. The following are definitions of common Usenet hierarchy addresses:

- ALT   for alternative topics
- COMP   for computer-science related topics
- MISC   for miscellaneous items
- REC   for recreation
- SCI   for science other than computers
- SOC   for social interaction and hobbies
- TALK   to talk to others

◈ **DejaNews - The Source for Internet Newsgroups**
http://www.dejanews.com/

◈ **Basic newsgroup and mailing list "Netiquette"**
http://www.herald.co.uk/
local_info/genuki/netiquette.html

Veronica and Jughead:

These programs function as indexes and search tools for Gopher sites. You can Telnet to these programs or use a browser to connect to a Gopher server that is running this type of software. Search engines on the WWW can also search for Gopher sites, so these indexing functions aren't necessarily as popular as they once were.

Virus:

A computer program or macro program created with the intent of causing harm or damage to computer programs and files. A virus can attach itself to another program or file on your computer. You can obtain a virus by sharing computer files with unreliable or unknown sources. Run a virus-scanning software program regularly to avoid accessing a virus.

◈ **Computer Virus Myths**
http://www.kumite.com/myths/

◈ **Don't Spread That Hoax!**
http://crew.umich.edu/~chymes/
Hoaxes/Think.html

◈ **U.S. Dept. of Energy Computer Incident Advisory Capability (CIAC)**
http://ciac.llnl.gov/ciac/
CIACHoaxes.html

◈ **Yahoo! - Computers - Viruses**
http://www.yahoo.com/
Computers_and_Internet/
Security_and_Encryption/Viruses/

Web Page:

A web page is a simple ASCII text file that is written using the language of the web - HTML or Hypertext Markup Language. A browser reads this file, interprets the language and displays the web page to you as the author intended. Several web pages make up a web site.

Web Site:

A web site is made up of more than one web page and is usually owned by one person or one group. Generally a web site will have a specific theme or purpose which is clearly displayed as you move from page to page within the site. Sometimes that theme or purpose might be as specific as German genealogy. Other times it may be that the whole site belongs to someone named Bob.

Webmaster:

The owner or person responsible for maintaining a web site. A webmaster creates and designs a web page, writes the HTML that makes up the page and uploads the page to the web server where it will be accessible to other Internet users. The webmaster is the person who updates the pages and keeps all information current. This is the person you would contact if you had any problems or found any errors on a web site.

Most often, in the case of a personal home page, this will also be the person you contact in order to share your genealogical information. Look throughout the web site in order to locate the name and e-mail address of this person.

WWW - World Wide Web, "The Web":

"The Web" has been around for several years, but has really taken off the last two years. A *home page* is the opening screen for a WWW site. The *URL* or address for a web site always starts with **http://** which stands for *Hypertext Transfer Protocol*. The web is a graphical interface to the Internet. It takes advantage of multimedia to bring home pages to life. Pages can include pictures, sound, movies, animations and more. You can navigate through web pages using hypertext links. These will appear on the web page as underlined text which is usually shown in a different color from the rest of the text. Just move your mouse to place the cursor over the hypertext link and click on these highlighted words to move to that link's web page. This method makes moving around the web quick and easy. Graphics can also be set up to be clickable links to other web pages. Pass your cursor over a *site map* or decorative graphic. If the cursor changes from an arrow to a hand with a pointing finger you know that graphic is a clickable link. For genealogists, there are some software packages available that will convert your genealogy software GEDCOM database file into HTML format in order to present the contents of the GEDCOM file on a web page. With your own home page, you can place your GEDCOM online for people to search any time, day or night, from anywhere in the world.

Index

virus scanning, 151
   definition, 172
zipped files, 43, 152

spam
   definition, 169
   misc. e-mail considerations, 47

surfing, surfin' the 'net
   definition, 169
   more than just web sites, 113
   tips and techniques for surfing
      success, 115

SYSOP
   definition, 169

TCP/IP (Transmission Control Protocol and Internet Protocol)
   definition, 169

Telnet
   definition, 170
   from a web browser, 113
   list of addresses, 85, 131, 146
   other options for genealogical
      research, 145, 146

thread
   definition, 170
   Deja News, 125
   mailing lists, 53
   newsgroups, 57, 73
      example, 74

tips and techniques
   e-mail, 43
   mailing lists and newsgroups, 74
   web, 115

tools you will need
   e-mail, 30
   Internet, 17
   mailing lists, 55
   web, 102

upload
   definition, 170
   e-mail, 36
      attachments, 42

URL
   bookmarks or favorites, 107, 117

copy and paste, 109
definition, 170
from search engines, 167
typing manually, 108

Usenet
   definition, 171
   Deja News, 124
   see *newsgroups*

USGenWeb
   census project description, 139
   research strategies, 126-127
   queries, 84
   URL, 133

vendors (books, software, maps, supplies, etc.)
   web sites, 140

Veronica
   definition, 171

virus
   definition, 172
   signature list, 154
   software, 151, 154

web
   browser, 103
      bookmarks or favorites, 107, 117
      definition, 158
      getting to know your browser, 103
      plug-ins, 112
      software, 20, 154
      toolbar and menu options, 104
   definition, 173
   examples of web sites currently
      available, 129
      Cyndi's List of Genealogy Sites on
        the Internet, 129
      libraries and archives, 131
      link lists, 133
      locality and ethnic specific sites,
        133
      personal home pages, 134
      research guides, tools and
        references, 136
      searchable databases and surname
        lists, 138
      societies and groups, 140
      vendors - books, software, maps,
        supplies, etc., 140
   FTP via a web page, 151